Mortgage Advising – The New Rules

How to be a successful UK Mortgage Adviser in the 2020s

Paul Archer

HH

High House Publishing

First published in Great Britain in 2022 by High House Publishing, Tivoli Studios, Cheltenham, UK

Printed and bound in Great Britain by Lulu.com.

Cover designed by Shelley White

ISBN 978-0-9933112-9-1 (Paperback)

For all your mortgage training needs, in-house requirements, contact Paul at:

paul@paularcher.com
www.paularcher.com
www.paularcher.uk
+44 (0)7702 341769

This book is dedicated to my wife Shelley and daughter Jess for supporting me throughout my journey and always offering advice, ideas, and inspiration to help me with my work. In addition, all the mortgage advisers I've worked with over the last 30 years of sales managing, coaching, training, and mentoring. You all embody a noble profession.

Table of Contents

How the World of Mortgage Advising Has Changed

What Are the Trends Driving Change?

All aspects of the economy have changed because of shifts happening around them. These shifts can be minor or global, but they drive change for any industry. The mortgage sector is no different. It is not immune to the shifts affecting the market and society.

It has been slower to evolve, though, compared to other sectors. Regulation, cartel-like operations, and reliance on traditional ways have slowed the sector's evolution. But change is accelerating. COVID has ensured that. The industry can't drag its heels anymore; it needs to move with the times.

The main trends which are driving the change are:

Population Growth

Which includes immigration. The UK now has more young people and families setting up eager to buy their first homes. On the opposite side, we have a massive Baby Boomer Generation retiring living in expensive piles of bricks, anxious to stay where they are and not downsize. Why should they?

The Housing Stock

Continues to grow very slowly. One initiative after another is creating more new housing, and ways of developing our existing stock are coming on stream. However, we have a limited supply. With a smaller landmass than many countries and one of the world's highest population densities – 276 people per square kilometre – this supply restriction will continue. This creates fizzy housing prices.

Regulation

Always upon us and constantly evolving. Regulation affects the entire lending market – unsecured and secured – plus equity release. Regulation stifles change and slows evolution down. But it protects the consumer, which is worth the restrictions.

The advice gap will shrink even further. Fewer people enter the advice market since regulation makes it hard to do so. The price of entry is high, so it puts many off. The regulator is aware of this and is trying to fix the problem. The answer is the automation of advice for those who can't afford or won't pay the high charges pursued in the financial sector. Automated advice will be low cost. This will effectively plug the advice gap.

The Lending Marketplace

The primary providers of mortgages – the banks and building societies – are already some way along their change curve. This is now having a remarkable effect on the provision of advice. The trend is that they are no longer talking to their millions of customers.

Branches closed many years ago and continue to fold. Head Office call centres are a nightmare to contact, and customers have lost faith in them. All their banking is now conducted on Smartphones. Banks no longer talk to customers, so they can't give advice or cross-sell anymore.

Constant mis-selling scandals from the 1990s to now have suffocated their desire to give advice and cross-sell products.

The trend is that these bodies are no longer providing the advice risk but still have plenty of money to lend, preferring to do this via brokers. They have war-chests of cash to lend and want to profit from this.

Soon, they will lend this money directly to consumers using Smartphone app technology and Artificial Intelligence to take the advice risk. They have the tech capability and motivation to lend and access large amounts of money.

This trend will persist and create the biggest challenges for brokers.

Technology

Always around us and ubiquitous. It will continue to affect the way brokers work.

Broadband Speed

Continues to improve. Landlines and fibre speeds are speeding up in most towns. Mobile broadband with 5G and 6G will allow exhilaratingly fast connection speeds. Not just in towns and cities but the wilderness too.

Couple this with Elon Musk's Starlink will mean geography has little bearing for the future. You will have just as fast broadband speed in the Hebrides as in Harlow. You don't need to be in an office to receive fast connections. We all now have them at home. And home may be in Bromley, Bhutan, or Boston.

Social Media

This is well documented and understood. Essentially, it's about people meeting up online rather than face to face. The trend is taking social media into the metaverse. The much-vaunted 3D virtual environment where people will meet online as though they are in the real world. The most significant driver of change – money – is in plenty of supply, bringing this trend to market.

More Knowledgeable Customers

This trend has been moving steadfastly over the last 20 years. The internet and a more comprehensive education system for our young people with university becoming the norm is the cause. Plus, newfound confidence that anything can be learnt.

Cloud Computing

Championed by the big tech firms in the early years of this century, notably Microsoft and Amazon, cloud computing is now dominant. It's beginning to affect our working lives. Thank goodness it has; otherwise, working from home during COVID would have been impossible. Cloud computing means we no longer have to be tethered to high powered server systems and office computers. We can work just as well on a laptop in our back garden.

Climate Change

The environment and global warming. The changing trend is not so much the actual warming of our earth and climate change resulting. This is alarming.

No, I refer to the acceptance of governments and the population to do something about it.

The World of Work

It is moving more towards smaller enterprises, self-employed, contracting rather than the lifetime job at the big corporation in the city. Work, in general, is not just being produced in central locations but all over.

Transparency

Freedom of information, Wiki leaks, the internet, government openness are all driving transparency. Nothing is kept secret anymore.

Cartels find it challenging to operate, and competition drives away their advantages. Just look at the abolition of unfair pricing in the general insurance market that has just recently been brought in by the FCA.

Prices are falling as competitors race to the bottom. Gravy trains are ending. Charges in pension and investment managed funds. Energy price cartels, food, hotel accommodation. The race to the bottom will continue.

Generation Z

Younger generations weaned on technology, aware of transformation and driving change. More accepting of new ways of doing things.

COVID

Will it ever go away, or will we be faced with continual variants and similar diseases from the animal kingdom? It's called zoonotic disease.

The trend is to embrace it, live with it and adapt our lifestyles to accommodate it, rather than fight it.

These are all hard trends, some softer than others and tricky to predict. Some are favourites and worth putting a tenner on. They are all evident right now and are driving change in our sector.

Let me now explain how these hard trends are affecting us.

How has the Mortgage Sector Changed?

Or is it currently changing? Let's talk about what we're seeing and what will happen in the mortgage advice sector driven by these trends.

In no particular order.

Money Available

There's plenty of money to lend, no shortage at all. Retail cash is currently available – post-COVID; this has been expanded dramatically with the British public hoarding all their lockdown money.

Wholesale cash is accessible, and properly executed mortgage-backed securities are holding their own in the money markets generating even more money to lend. This is currently causing more lenders to appear. Challenger banks and small specialised lenders are appearing weekly.

The specialised lenders are cropping up, armed with their team of Business Development Managers poached from the banks; they are eager to lend. This competition in money loosens lending criteria making it easy to satisfy your client demands. Lower rates as margins are squeezed, and the broker's role becomes even more demanding.

This trend will drive the attraction of mortgage brokers who can search the marketplace mainly for specialised products. The newer breed of lenders are not vanilla; they are specialists able to charge extra interest for buy to lets, development finance and such lending.

Vanilla lending is not their bag.

Disintermediation

Everyone struggles with this term when studying for their CeMAP. It now seems increasingly out of date. Having banks to collect savings and lend them out as a middleman appears very 1990's

Why do we need banks to obtain the money, package this into a mortgage and make this available? Why can't we source the money from the markets, create our own mortgages and tailor these to individual customers? Brokers, possibly the larger ones, may do this in the future and offer bespoke mortgage packages specifically designed for that client. The role of the banks may come to a grinding halt.

Banks No Longer Advising

At every opportunity, the banks are shaving their advice teams. Moving them from closed branches initially and now culling their telephony teams and video advisers. This will continue. They currently spend more on business development managers than their advising teams.

They are more interested in convincing brokers to lend their money and have huge budgets to encourage them. Just look at the awards dinners and industry events sponsored in their thousands by the banks to attract brokers to their stands.

Make hay whilst the sun shines. There is reasonable proc fees and cheap lending to secure for your clients. Currently, only brokers can do this unless the customer goes direct.

Arti et Al

Going direct to a bank is currently fraught with processes and red-tape and requires immense patience. That's changing. The likes of Arti are ensuring customers who go direct are now being looked after by artificial intelligence.

Alexa type apps can help people obtain their cheap mortgages direct from banks. This is getting better each day; more younger people are flocking to them via their trusted Smartphones. The banks love this because they can lend directly again and reap all the margin as profits with little expense.

Eventually, they will not need brokers and stop paying proc fees; this isn't far away, and you need to prepare now.

Evolution of the AR Model

The mortgage world is not immune to outside change, and the drift towards self-autonomy ripples into our world. This is also driven by regulatory requirements and the distinct lack of large mortgage advice firms.

Larger firms are more inclined to take on the risk of employing new advisers and affording the considerable cost of training and developing them. The banks used to do this and do it very well. But they've pulled out.

Experienced advisers are filling the few employed positions available, leaving the experience of self-employment the only route for new advisers. The FCA is worried because most principal firms and networks use the appointed representative (AR) model to take on self-employed brokers.

The regulator's fear stems from the fact that some of these principals are not providing sufficient support and oversight. Training, development, supervision, and coaching ensure the new person becomes an excellent adviser. This part is expensive in money and people. Expect the FCA to win this battle – they generally do.

Expect the AR model to evolve – after all, it is a throwback to the first regulation in 1988 and has changed very little.

Nobody knows how it will change. For me, I think there will be more employed positions emanating from smaller brokers as the regulator makes the onboarding process more manageable. In addition, a drift towards larger advice firms taking on the reigns of bringing in new people for training and development. They have the budgets and know-how.

They may replace the role of the banks. Besides, many individuals like the safety of a corporate environment, having a line manager and a coach who has your back and the security and growth potential of being part of a large business.

Larger Advice Firms

Private equity money and City investments allow firms to become more prominent, grander, and corporate. The vacuum left by the banks will be filled by these firms. Already two or three large networks are being valued weekly in the press. It is a sure sign that they will go to the market as a PLC or obtain private investment to grow big.

Large advice firms will begin to dominate the market. They can drive costs down and do things on a scale smaller brokers can't. We used to call it "stack 'em high and sell 'em cheap".

Mortgage advice will follow this model. Low-cost operations, utilising the latest technology to advise, will be their forte. They will bring in new blood. Train and develop the newer breed of advisers to populate the sector. They will have unique brands unbloodied by past mis-selling scandals, and their apps will appeal to the general public.

Most of their work will be in the vanilla space where mortgages can be arranged quickly, painlessly, and profitably. They will take preferred adviser status from the suppliers of lending money and receive enhanced proc fees for the volume they produce. Ultimately they may go straight to the markets for wholesale money and create their own lending.

Competition from AI Apps

The broker community has always provided ample competition to the consumer's benefit. Contentiously this might be a cosy cartel.

Proc fees are agreed upon at the lender level, and most brokers receive the same amount. Commissions are set by insurers, and everyone gets pretty much the same. Other incentives payable to brokers are heavily regulated except the Award Dinner extravaganza and free bars.

Broker fees are set by brokers, but competition keeps these tamed.

The cost of entry to the broker world is high.

That's about to change with the rise of the AI Apps or Bots that will give mortgage advice in the future. We've already spoken about this. These apps, run by the larger advice firms and lenders direct, will provide sound advice for simple cases to begin with.

They will learn quickly and will offer more complex advice in the future. They are cheap and will charge no fee. They are clever in that they can talk to all other computer systems in the house buying process, speeding up everything. The lawyer's computer system via APIs, open banking for bank current account data, social media feeds for a fact-find, land registry for the property, valuation data for surveys, credit scores and lender data for the loan amounts. And so on.

They will be lightning-fast at applications – DIPs in seconds, full factfinds in no time, mortgage apps submitted over the wire, insurance apps via electronic means. Completion in days rather than weeks.

Rather than face these apps head-on at their own game, you'll want to plan to work alongside them as well as offer an advice service that the apps can't do. You can't directly compete.

Regulation and the Advice Gap

No significant changes are envisaged. The polarisation of permission may change. Essentially different advice areas require separate approvals from the regulator. This causes a silo effect but makes it easier for the regulator to oversee the sector and advice given.

The regulator is acutely aware that the advice gap is widening. They are supporting automation of advice which will soak up this gap. Automation models may be allowed to garner several permissions to operate. Ironically this may pave the way for a seismic change or a throwback to the old.

Technology and AI Apps will be taking care of much of the uncomplicated and straightforward advice the masses need. This leaves mortgage advisers open to providing personalised service to their clients. More advanced specialised service allows mortgage advisers to gain more permissions – equity release, long term care, protection, and ultimately pension and wealth management.

Successful brokers will move into specialised lending situations as the AI Apps will deal with vanilla. Complex cases, curious income models, special financing.

Equity release will explode as the Baby Boomers all retire and yearn to pass on their property wealth to their children and straight to their grandchildren. This will help younger generations with much-needed deposits. These baby boomers will die and pass on their entire wealth, and the amounts of money predicted are eye-watering. Enough to satisfy the fee pockets of wealth managers for years to come.

This brings on the next phase in change – transparency.

Transparency

There are no monopoly practises in financial services, and one of the regulator's objectives is to encourage competition. Oddly though, current regulation does cause a few informal cartels. A cartel can be deliberate, such as OPEC, which controls oil supply to the world and thus the price.

Cartels can be informal, and they are inherent in our sector. Proc fees from lenders are kept to similar levels because the lenders have a cartel. Commission rates are similar. Regulation creates this. The most insidious cartel is related to wealth management fees. Or funds under management fees.

The wealth management sector relies on managing as much money as it can. This wealth is placed into funds of various guises. These funds are actively managed professionally by fund managers. These fund managers are paid handsomely. The wealth managers who direct the money to these funds also receive a generous percentage.

These percentages of funds under management is how wealth managers are paid. Few physically take a fee from clients. They do so by extracting a small portion of the funds under control. Half a per cent, one per cent may seem tiny but apply this to millions of pounds under management, and the fees become tantalisingly high.

The secret is that they provide active management. Their client's wealth increases because good decisions are made by knowledgeable and trained individuals. You can't argue with this.

The cartel is in place because no one wealth manager wants to reduce their percentages. Who would?

The threat to this cosy cartel is passive management. This is where funds are managed by computer AI. Algorithms and artificially intelligent software that manages the funds passively. In other words, where no humans are involved. This has dramatically reduced the funds' percentages, and the providers of these funds are arguing successfully that their passive models outperform humans. So, this is where the funds are migrating to and will end the gravy chain of active management charges.

Online Communications

This is where most mortgage advisers will see a revolution in their marketplace. Some already have because of the COVID working from home (WFH) explosion. But as WFH oscillates between mandatory and preferred, the number of complete converts to the model has shrunk. Still, many advisers see this model as the future. Not so much working from home but the use of video communications rather than face to face meetings. Or at least a hybrid of the two.

Contemporary advisers are embracing technology and doing it very well. Many are evolving their sales processes to accompany the video model. Shorter and more often. 20 minutes here and 20 minutes there rather than the extended 90-minute face to face meeting, with lots of cups of tea and rapport.

Home is not always the right place to give advice. Still, suppose a dedicated office space can be sought with the right tech. In that case, an adviser can talk to clients in a very professional manner. Some are creating studios or advice centres from their offices which have faster, more reliable broadband and an air of professionalism. This also allows for a hybrid approach, so some meetings can be face to face and others online. All operated from the same base.

Cloud computing and fast home broadband, plus space, can have this operation emanating from the home. We will see this more as the future evolves. Apart from freedom and work/life balance, the main driver is the lower cost. Advisers competing with low-cost models reduce their overheads. How best to do this than disposing of the expensive office and having everyone virtual.

When operating virtually, you can work from anywhere in the world. Regulators might have something to say about this, but if you're authorised and compliant, why can't you operate from Cyprus or Canada? Or at least in the Scottish Highlands as opposed to expensive London. This all drives down costs.

The Metaverse

The metaverse may gain traction. It may not. With bottomless pockets and the desire to defend advertising revenue, tech firms will drive the metaverse with social media dominating. Advisers will use it if their clients embrace it. I think they will – clients, especially as the metaverse becomes mainstream accessed via a Smartphone.

This is a total game-changer and ticks all the boxes of the occurring changes. We're already using it to deliver training and coaching – if we can, so can you.

Technology

The tech evolution is well documented and doesn't need me to add more commentary. Progressive advisers, particularly new ones, embrace tech from day one and automate everything they do. When faced with a challenge, think about how tech can solve the problem. New hardware or software to drive the business forward. Modern advisers use tech to do the heavy lifting.

A building firm will bring in mechanised equipment to clear a site and dig trenches with one man operating the vehicle. Soon a robot machine will emulate the same job, and a person will view the results afterwards, tweaking the trench size etc.

Likewise, a mortgage brokerage will use tech to factfind the client and draw up some initial advice, utilising social media feeds to populate the client's details. Extracting data using open banking, seeking updates from computer links. The adviser then sits down with the results, tweaks them and communicates it all to the client, who trusts them, not the machine.

Open-minded advisers will work with tech to help clients with their financial needs, using software to do the parts of the job that don't require them anymore. They will not fight against it but use it instead.

Caring For Our Environment

Possibly the change that will drive everything. This requirement is being driven by social influence, money and government incentives. It must succeed if we wish to leave a world to our children; it's a simple as that.

Everything that advisers do in the future will have one eye on the environment. Advisers will be measuring their carbon footprint, clients will demand this, and society will compel it. Using petrol-driven cars to drive to a client's house versus an electric vehicle or even a video meeting. CPD from a hotel conference room 200 miles away versus online learning. Networking online or in the metaverse versus train journeys and tube trips to an office block in central London. Compelling clients to drive to your pristine offices and park in town just to meet you on your Chesterfield sofa?

Awards dinners in central Manchester. BDMs travel hundreds of hours each month just to visit a broker in their office because they prefer to? Staff working from home or pressganged into attending an office each day?

All these decisions have to be made with the environment in mind, not just money or because it's the way we've always done it. Or that clients want to meet face to face. Or I operate better in an office.

Achievement Goal Setting For Your Mortgage Business

Chapter Summary

2021 was the impact of the one in a lifetime "Black Swan" event - COVID 19. No one saw it coming, and it has revolutionised the mortgage advice sector for those who wish to move forwards.

2022 and onwards has the potential for innovation, opportunities, and achievement. There are so many ideas you've heard from your mentors, so much to do but so little time.

The answer is to clearly set out your goals. Identifiable and stimulating goals lead to a pathway of quarterly objectives to help you take your mortgage practice to the heights you envisage.

This chapter will show you my goal-setting blueprint to succeed in 2022 and beyond. Having used this goal-setting strategy every year since 1995, I have established and grown my own training business and adapted and innovated with the times.

Here's the blueprint:

Long-Term Vision

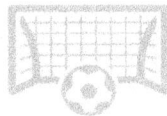
Annual Goals

Quarterly Objectives

Strategic Next Actions (SNAs)

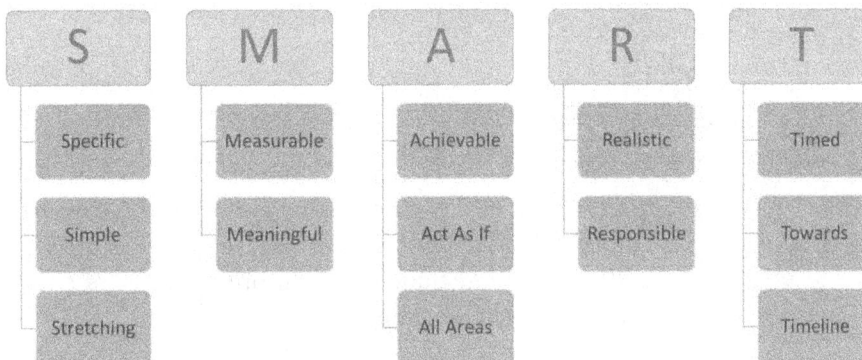

Long Term Visioning

We start with long term visioning. How long is long? Well, that's entirely up to you. Some people set lifelong goals; however, life can be too unpredictable, so 5 years suit me. I've set long term visions every 5th year since 1996, and they are eerily accurate.

During my first NLP training in London, I set my first goal. It related to setting up my own consultancy business. As NLP likes to call it, my well-formed outcome was sitting in my home office opening a letter and inside was a cheque from a client settling an invoice in full. I vividly remember in late 2000 opening an envelope with my son Euan by my side, with a cheque from the Bradford and Bingley for some training I did for them that summer.

A vision I set in 2015 was standing in front of a large monitor presenting to hundreds of people across the world via the internet. Ironically 5 years later, in the height of the first lockdown, I found myself standing in front of an extensive computer monitor teaching sales skills to salespeople in the USA.

You don't need to know how these are going to be fulfilled. Set the goal with your conscious cognitive mind and let fate or your unconscious figure out how to achieve them. And it will so long as you plant it well in your timeline. More on well-formed outcomes, timelines and NLP later, but next, let's get into annual goal setting.

Vision Boards

But before we go, the last word on Vision Boards. I like these and have used them from time to time as people are inherently visual in their make-up. A goals board or vision board consists of a poster-sized print full of pictures and visuals depicting your vision. Cutouts from magazines usually represent physical wants such as a new car or a detached house in the country. The constant reminder of seeing your board on your kitchen wall can be stimulating and very motivational.

It also cements my thinking that visions and long-term goals can be planted in the conscious mind but left to the unconscious mind to figure out how to get there.

Set SMART Annual Goals

I'm sure you may have read or heard about SMART goals and objectives. Google it, and you'll find numerous resources on the topic as it is well received and accepted.

Goals need to be set each calendar year. I'm writing this just before Christmas, and I'll be penning my goals over the holidays. You should do too. These goals should be SMART but not SMART as you know it. My SMART includes a few more parameters that will help you pen and form really well-formed outcomes or goals.

Many of these goals or annual objectives need to be vigorously planned. A series of strategic actions are laid out to achieve them. They don't need to be left to the unconscious to sort out. You need a plan, and every goal needs quarterly actions and mini objectives to achieve them. I call these Strategic Next Actions or SNAs, which evolve from goals.

Let's get into how we formulate these goals with our SMART method.

S – Specific, Simple and Stretching

Specific

A specific goal is detailed and readily determined. The more specific, the better. It may become more of a vision than a goal if it's too big and global. There's nothing wrong with those, but we're looking at yearly goals here, not lifetime ambitions.

The trick is to learn chunk sizes. Chunk sizes come from NLP and allow you to recognise if something is a big chunk or small. The aim is to get the goal as specific as possible, so we need to chunk them down. Try asking yourself the question: "to achieve this goal, what's getting in the way?".

The resulting answers will become mini-goals to allow you to achieve the bigger goal. You've successfully chunked it down.

The other issue about a specific goal is how it's defined. For example, many people want to have an income goal for their business and express this vaguely. Is it profit, turnover, salary, bonus or growth? It's good, to be exact.

Simple

Simple allows you to quickly figure out how to achieve it. The goal should be simply stated to determine your strategic next actions (SNAs) rather than using high convoluted words that just confuse.

Stretching

Finally stretching. Some people call it exciting, others stretching. This makes sense as a goal should get those motivational chemicals mixing in your mind. Still, not all goals can excite, particularly if they're annual business goals. Welcome to the real world. However, a stretching goal makes logical sense and can help you achieve great results. The secret is to get a balance.

For my 50th birthday, I was given a three-hour excursion with a Police Traffic Officer in his speedy Volvo. Was I excited? The first lesson was how to control a car whilst skidding, then he taught us how to drive fast. The finale of the class was to take the wheel of his hideously fast Volvo and go as fast as I could along a public motorway. I tell you, I was scared.

A friend of mine came along to keep me company, and this was great as we could make mistakes together and not feel so bad. But to make a mistake when driving at more than

100mph on a public highway could be dangerous. Very dangerous. "You take the wheel first," said the policeman. "And take us as fast as you can, but don't forget what I taught you." Great advice, especially the negative, so my brain immediately forgot everything he taught me.

But I knew a bit about setting goals, so I told myself that I would exceed 115mph. I knew my limits!

Off I went cruising at 70mph. "OK," said the policeman. "Let's take it up". And off I went 80... 90... 100mph... 110... 118mph. Was I thrilled? Safe and relieved, I slowed down and let my friend David have a go.

Within a minute, he was doing 136mph. I asked him afterwards how he managed it. David said that after I'd gone first and he could see himself going faster than me, it was now more manageable.

So, stretch your goals – you'll be amazed at what you are capable of. Instead of focusing around 115mph, I should have targeted myself for 130. Just that little bit faster.

M – Measurable and Meaningful

Measurable

Most business textbooks will show you how to measure your objectives and goals. Metrics, Key Performance Indicators (KPIs), performance measures are all things you should do. The oldest adage is what gets measured gets done and is true in business.

These kinds of measurements are great for performance objectives and strategies. But some goals are challenging to measure objectively.

For example, you may set a goal to achieve £100,000 of net profit for your business this year. That's easily measured; just ask your accountant. Of course, there will be some complexities, but relatively simple to measure the success.

However, not every goal shall be written this way. As we shall discuss later in this piece, there's more to success than just a monetary value. There's your health. What would happen if you achieved this goal and accomplished burnout in your mental health?

Well-Formed Outcomes

Let me share with you another measurement tactic that'll allow you to know when you've achieved a relatively chunky goal. This method works well with reasonably big goals. It's a "sledgehammer for a nut" solution for most goals you set in your mortgage business.

Let me explain how it works.

A well-formed outcome is your goal. NLP calls it this, and I like it. Rather than setting a goal set in the future, you write one that has already been done. A well-formed outcome that you can already see, feel, hear, smell and possibly taste. My example from earlier with the cheque was a well-formed outcome.

When I set the goal, I imagined the situation in the future when I had achieved the goal. The timescale was largely flexible, but I clearly defined precisely when I had accomplished the goal.

Written in the present tense as opposed to the future. I'm sitting on my office chair, in my study, opening an envelope. It's daylight outside; the postman has just delivered. My children are around me; everyone is happy and healthy. I'm relaxed, worthy and humble as I open the envelope to reveal a cheque written by a client in full settlement for some work carried out.

I'm clear to what I can see, hear. I know how I feel. Smell and taste are not involved, but that's OK, and I'm using all the senses to predict the outcome. It's easy to imagine, and I keep reminding myself what it looks like. Every time I picture the scene, it gets increasingly accurate in my minds' eye until it becomes completely believable.

When it happened on that September day in 2000, Euan wasn't in the picture, so I invited him in from the playroom to see what Daddy was up to. The goal was achieved, and the outcome became real. Pretty uncanny, you might say, but totally accurate. That's the power of well-formed outcomes. They're also effortless to measure and not a metric in place.

Meaningful

Meaningful is my second M. This is important and provides further motivation, another M, but we have enough of those. Meaningful relates to the concept that the goal is yours and doesn't belong to anyone else. Is it significant for you or benefits a third party who has influenced you to set the goal?

The best example is a career goal set by your parents when you left Uni or College. Did you really want to be a corporate lawyer working all the hours in the city? Or was it more meaningful for your parents? Now pleasing your parents is a noble objective, but setting a goal to achieve something that has little meaning to yourself will only end in unhappiness someday.

A – Achievable, Act As If, All Areas

Achievable

Three for you under the A.

Achievable has done the rounds plenty of times and is often criticised for directly contrasting with making your goal stretching. Suppose your question is that the goal you're setting is not achievable. In that case, you will dilute it to suit your current opinions of your capability. Your limiting beliefs may drag you down, and that's a huge shame. If you think this affects your achievements, do work on these first.

Sometimes having a goal with no idea how to achieve it spurs you on because you will figure out how to do it.

I admire people who say I've set this goal or that goal, but I'm not sure how to do it yet. It probably won't be too difficult. I can learn how to do that; I'll figure it out shortly.

Act As If

As if, is far more motivational and inspirational too. Act as if you have already achieved it takes you to a different plane. Express your goal "as if" you've done it. A little like my cheque and envelope story from earlier. Present tense the vocabulary. "I am here" or "I do this" or "I earn this".

All Areas of Your Life

All areas of your life ensure you balance your goals. Whenever I set my annual goals, I always ensure my personal life, welfare, fitness, relationships are all catered for in my goals. I'm not a machine; I'm a human who has multiple areas of my life that link together like a jigsaw.

My health, for example, will affect my work ethic. My fitness influences the energy I must have to perform in front of 100 people. They are connected. After the famous cowboy film starring Yul Brinner and countless other stars, I call the areas the Magnificent Seven.

These are my 7 key areas you may want to set your annual goals. In no particular order:

1. Personal development goals – your CPD and "saw sharpening" activities

2. Revenue goals for your mortgage advising business

3. Maximising technology in your business

4. Business generation goals

5. Health, welfare, fitness and spiritual goals

6. Family, friends and social goals

7. Publishing and content creation goals

You may wish to add some categories that suit you. Some people add relationship goals and materialist goals. The choice is yours but be aware that these are annual goals and haven't yet been converted to objectives that you can achieve each quarter.

R – Realistic, Responsible

Realistic

Realistic has done the rounds for many years on goal setting. Not to be confused with achievable, realistic is all about how real it is for you personally. Are you 100% convinced it'll happen? What degree of certainty do you have to ensure it'll be achieved?

Responsible

Responsible is where it's at. You're personally responsible for the goal happening and the impact it has. Everything in life has a cause and an effect. The cause is you achieving the goal, the effect can be seen in three areas:

1. For example, you – your health or damaged mental health – reached a goal that completely burnt you out.

2. Others – how much effect did your goal have on other people. Who did you upset along the way, who was damaged by it? For example, you were so ruthless

in getting the goal nailed before the year-end you hurt your partner or didn't give them the attention they needed at the time. You were too laser-focused to the detriment of others.

3. The Planet – enough said. That fast car you wanted was built on a 4-litre fuel-injected engine that destroyed your carbon footprint.

T – Timed, Towards

Timed

Or timescale. This is where you put some date or time for when your goal needs to be achieved. Day, date and time all help. Is it next year, or will it never arrive?

One of the most potent time-based elements to goal setting is establishing your timeline and planting the goal inside your timeline when it is achieved. We talked about this earlier and will revisit it very shortly. But next comes towards.

Towards

Towards is a another NLP'ism. One of the meta programmes, an awful title, but very impactful. People see things along a spectrum of towards or away from. Some motivation is focused on achieving things in the future, striving for a goal heading towards something.

On the other end of the spectrum is away from. Away from is propelling yourself away from something to achieve a goal. For example, losing weight, not failing in business, or leaving the current relationship. Goal setting works best towards goals since we generally get what we set out for. Losing weight can be converted to gaining a meaningful frame or squeezing into speedos on summer holidays.

More powerful.

Timeline Goal Setting

This is one of those techniques that you must try to embrace. It does sound a tad whacky. On my first timeline exercise back in the 1990s, they called it timeline therapy. Now, if that's not enough to put you off doing something serious and grown-up, I don't know what will.

But it worked; I was hooked. So I want to share with you how it works and how it'll deliver significant advantages in having some of your larger, hairier goals come true.

The first step is to believe this can work.

The second step is to discover your imaginary timeline. Ask yourself the question, "if you were to point to where your time goes forward, then point now."

Now show me where your time comes from.

Join the two together, and you have a timeline. Showing the past (probably behind you) and the future (definitely in front of you).

Next, you want to be able to float in your timeline just like you swim in a swimming pool. This is purely imaginary, and people like to relax and do this. Some folks want to close their eyes, but that's up to you. Floating along your timeline is very therapeutic; you can see and feel all the history and take a glance at your future too.

Now, let's get into the setting and planting goals. The concept is that you create and define your goal, then pop it into the future as though it has been achieved. Let me demonstrate, and you can follow me with your own goal.

Timeline Demonstration

I have an important goal for 2022: to get involved as part of the team running the Professional Speaking Association (PSA) Virtual Chapter to benefit new and existing PSA members. I've been a member of the PSA since its inauguration in the UK in 1999. I have gained from all those years of self-development, ideas and creativity. I want to pay back, so to speak and aid members in running their speaking businesses virtually.

It's one of those goals where some planning is needed but a fair bit of serendipity. So, I will plant this in my timeline to ensure I achieve it. Behind me is the past, and my future is directly in front of me. Remember, this is purely a metaphor to help your mind's eye.

As I float upwards into my timeline like the Jetstream in the Northern Hemisphere, I surge forward in its wake as soon as I enter it. My future is panning out underneath me; I can see what's going on as I flow forward. I stop moving forward when I reach the moment when I've achieved the goal. Next, I float downwards into my body at the exact moment the goal has been reached. Inside my own body, I want to check around me to get a feel for what's happened.

What do I see, feel, hear, smell, taste?

This is my well-formed outcome. I'm sitting on my stool in my studio, looking into the primary camera. In front of me, I have my four monitors where I can see all the audience on Zoom. It's early evening but dark outside, so probably autumn. We're all laughing; something has happened to make us chuckle. I think we're celebrating our inaugural session of the PSA Virtual Chapter. I feel excited and motivated. Who else is with me? Shelley is upstairs listening in.

That's the well-formed outcome; I'm not sure exactly when it is, but it's in my timeline, and it didn't take too long to get there, so probably about 9 months or so away.

Next, I float out of my body up into the timeline and return to the current day. As I come back, I look down at all the things I've done to achieve my goal. All the small actions I've taken to progress, all the calls I've made, people I've spoken to, things I've done. There's a lot to do, but I'm letting my mind know what they are.

I return to my current time and pop back into my body.

I've planted the outcome into my timeline. Every opportunity I have, I will repeat the exercise to cement the goal in my timeline and embed all the actions into my subconscious.

You create and set the goal using your conscious mind and let the subconscious decide how it will be achieved.

Converting Annual Goals to Quarterly Objectives

Now you have all your annual goals. Mine are always in a mindmap because it helps me keep them all on one sheet. The mindmap has the categories I use. These are my focus points for the year and contain the goals.

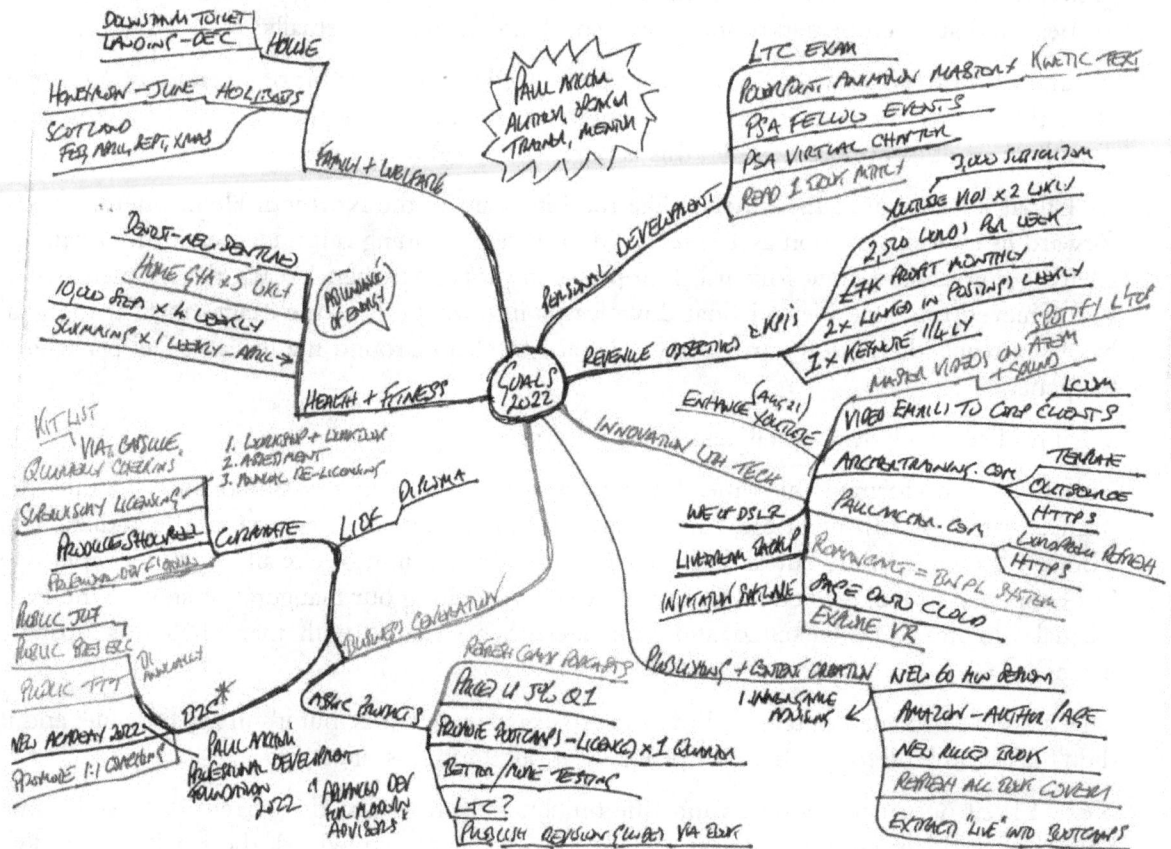

I divide the year into quarters – Q1, Q2, Q3 and Q4, so I start in January at the beginning of the year with Q1. It's nothing more complicated than scanning what else is going on in the quarter and then determining which of my goals I want to get done in that quarter.

I suppose these are now more objectives than goals, but I'm not going to wax lyrical about the difference; it doesn't really matter.

Objectives and Strategic Next Actions (SNAs)

As the months evolve, I need to set tactics and strategies to achieve the goals. They're done via SNAs – or Strategic Next Actions. SNAs are those bit tasks or actions that step you towards attaining the goal.

Using my example of the PSA Virtual Chapter. SNAs will be talking to guest speakers, getting members for the chapter, emailing members, deciding on the structure of sessions, etc. These are just run of the mill actions that need to be done – I call them SNAs. This one is a self-development goal, so it is called SNA:CPD.

This indicates that they are actions towards that goal group.

Other SNAs I have are:

- SNA:CPD
- SNA:Fee
- SNA:Tech
- SNA:BizDev
- SNA:Personal
- SNA:Writing

Now not every SNA will be towards a goal, but most are. It's a great way to ensure all your actions have a purpose and move you forward in your business. I use an SNA:Admin for everyday admin tasks in my task list.

Colour Coding Your Diary

Our strategic next actions are clearly defined by our goals, and you really shouldn't do anything that doesn't contribute to those goals. However, the real-world kicks in, and we do end up reacting and doing tasks that are not directly relevant but need doing.

To keep these in check, it's often an excellent idea to colour code your calendar so you can see whether you are on track or not.

Here's my suggestion:

- Red – making money

- Blue – marketing activities

- Yellow – administration

- Green – self-development

- Orange – personal activities.

You can then see at a glance whether you're being productive or not:

Clearing Your Inbox Daily

Let's tame your email once and for all; I've known advisers to drown in it. Here's how.

You can check email regularly for essential items, but it's best to do this every couple of hours – say 9am, 12 noon, 3pm and 5pm. But only to deal with urgent ones, leave the rest till later when you clear your inbox.

For a quick reminder of urgent versus important, you won't do worse than Stephen Covey's Time Management Grid. You can see below that he creates four boxes that determine whether a task should be done or delayed, or even ignored

You must clear your inbox every day. Here's how.

Choose a 60 minute window every day at some time, best before the close of play. Start with the first email. Can you handle it in less than 2 minutes? If so, address it. If it takes longer than 2 minutes, then put it into a task to be dealt with at another time.

If you don't want something, such as a subscription, see if you can unsubscribe. Be ruthless with these.

If it just needs filing somewhere, just drag it into the folder on your PC where it belongs.

Work your way through your emails in this manner, and you will clear your inbox. And you must do this every day. Believe me, you'll feel good when you do.

Summary

Setting and achieving your goals is an essential task to be conducted annually. This has been my blueprint which you can freely use to maximise your mortgage business.

Advising the Generations – Matures, Boomers, X and Y

Why Generational Selling?

Saturday, shopping mall, my wife, credit cards hot with use…not my most enjoyable experience.

But for the sake of harmony, I need to endure these moments periodically, so how do I cope? Easy.

I comatose myself from the shopping experience and watch salespeople in action instead, noting positive and negative actions and skills. It's great fun.

This week I was fixed on the issue of selling to the four different generations. People from all four generations were shopping gleefully in the shopping mall, and how did the salespeople handle them?

Pretty much the same, which brought about some success and intense frustration on both fronts.

The plain fact is, we have to adapt our way of selling or handling customers. One way to achieve success is to segment them according to the four recognised generations.

So let me explore with you the four generations who will most likely be looking for mortgage or later-life lending advice.

- Matures born before 1945

- Baby Boomers – born 1945 to 1965

- Generation X – born 1965 to 1980

- Generation Y – born 1980 to 2000

Who Are the Generations?

Matures

Matures are mostly into retirement now and have a very traditional, cautious attitude to buying. They look for consistency and quality in their products and aim to buy services that are tried and tested by others before them. They are, and were, extremely loyal to the companies they work for and the companies they enjoy the products of.

They're living much longer than anticipated and need income to finance their spare time and, of course, long term care. The medicine popping generation spends more on healthcare than any other generation.

Baby Boomers

Baby Boomers are competitive, very hard working and tend to be in high levels of authority in the economy. They are, as such, the wealthiest spending generation, many sitting on high valued properties and assets, particularly equities and funds. They like to have trophies showing their hard work and success, and they want their products to demonstrate this success. Some have taken to technology, and some haven't.

The Baby Boomers win hands down; they're loaded as far as wealth is concerned. Sitting on vast property and asset wealth. Many are retired and living off their final salary pensions and investments.

Generation X

Generation X are quite different. The forgotten or bewildered generation. Financial scandal after scandal has affected the trust of corporations and salespeople. Their boom years were in the nineties and naughties, then brutally cut down to size with the credit crunch. They believe in property, and many have substantial wealth in this area, but also sizeable mortgages, considerable interest only.

The live for the moment generation have maxed their credit cards in more ways than one. Faced with alarmingly large university fees for their children and none of the significant company benefits that the Boomers enjoyed, they have justification for feeling hard done by. And jealous of the Boomers who enjoyed Woodstock and flower power, the 80's boom years and always seemed to have it their way.

They have substantial protection needs and retirement planning goals. No longer, members of final salary schemes feel abandoned by the pension authorities.

Generation Y

Finally, Generation Y. The eldest is in their early 40's, so they haven't had time to build up a store of wealth. An exciting generation, IT literate, multi-tasking, always on and instant gratification requirements stereotype them. Helicopter parented, attention-seeking and individuality yearning, that's the Generation Y.

Selling to Matures

Matures have an in built need to conform. They don't need to "rock the boat" or show their individuality like the Generation Ys. So they'll often go with the off the shelf solution only so long as it's tried and tested and oozes quality. No need to create tailored packages or solutions with the Matures.

Brought up with the rationing of war and post-war austerity, Matures value quality and want whatever they buy to last and be proven. They're not going to take up anything experimental, the latest fad. They respect proven quality and desire testimonials and referrals backing up our quality statements.

Communicate with them the old-fashioned way – face to face visit is always welcomed, meetings, phone calls and letters. Ask about other mediums; some have taken to email and other electronic communications, most haven't. Matures are not time-strapped like different generations; they are mostly all retired, so have the time to chat with you face to face or on the phone.

Follow the traditional sales process taught in sales training school as the Matures will adhere to this conformity. Earn the right to present your solution by building a rapport, showing your credentials, referring to the mighty organisation behind you (if you have one). Matures generally have a fondness and trust for large institutions, the government, charities, the church. Traditional institutions give them a warm feeling.

Be prepared to work hard during the sales process. Matures are comfortable and willing to follow the whole sales process. They will allow you to sell only when you've covered the correct ground previously. Remember to ask for the sale, matures expect you to ask and will reward you with loyal business if you've been successful.

Earn their respect and trust first, share your experiences and above all, ask them how they like to be treated and handled; they all have a way for you to sell to them. Stick to it.

Under promise and over deliver is a good handle to use with Matures. They are looking to trust you, and delivering on your promises within the timescales is vital.

Keep in touch with your Mature clients more than other generations. They don't get email inbox fever, so use the postal system to make contact. Newspapers, information, birthday cards are all very acceptable.

Selling to the Baby Boomers

Boomers are ambitious and competitive want to win and be successful. They want to show this success in material trappings. Conspicuous consumption is quite common as they show how successful they are by having something slightly better than everyone else. Just take a look at the board's car parking zone in corporate Britain. Cars show their wealth and position.

You need to be subtle but don't hold back on stroking their egos a little to air their hard work and success.

Known for their work ethic, Boomers will also expect this from you. So don't hide your workload on their behalf. Make visible what's usually visible – the long hours, the reports, the meetings, the decisions – all on their behalf. Make sure they know you're working hard for them and going the extra mile to secure their business. You'll be rewarded.

Use technology appropriately with Boomers. Many have adopted it and are using it progressively. You need to ask about their use and then match it but adopt traditional communication methods such as face-to-face time and telephone calls. Bear in mind that boomers are adopting the technology in their droves now that it's all getting more accessible. Smartphones and iPads that are always on and simple to operate are ticking their boxes. So be prepared to use modern technology to communicate more in the future.

Boomers like to fill their days with activities from work and home. This is the generation with the work/life balance predicament; other generations don't seem to be too troubled by it. The reason is that they want to be the best parent possible for their children, to give them the face time they want, the "me" time. They're constantly driving them to swimming lessons, brownies and Judo and have big ambitions for their university education.

They like to be busy. It's a sign of success. Remember, they have always been surrounded by many other boomers, so one way of being picked for promotion was to put in the long hours. As a result, they are busy, so anything you can do with your product to save them time is most welcomed. Look for time-saving angles and automated offerings that preserve their valuable spare time.

Boomers are not resistant to traditional sales practices in the same way as Matures. So approach them how you were trained – open, rapport, needs, solution and close – will work admirably with Boomers.

Coupled with time, Boomers like to control not as fetishlike as Generation X, but they want to know that things can be done. They look for features that give them this control, help them prioritise, and provide efficiency.

Having been brought up around many other Boomers, they are very comfortable in teams. Teamwork achieves excellent results. So, make your product appear part of a team. Ensure they know about all the other people on your team who are contributing to the value you're providing.

Remember your common courtesies with Boomers. Beware slang language and hip terms; they don't like them. Don't be overly casual or familiar unless you know them well.

Optimism, positivity, visible emotions are evident in Boomers. They were brought up to show their feelings, unlike Matures and the younger Generation X and Y's. Ensure you share this optimism and emotion when dealing with the Boomer. A can-do attitude will serve you well.

Selling to Generation X

So how do you sell to a Gen X? You don't, not in the traditional manner; if you do, you'll fail. Instead, let them buy on their terms and in their timescale. Don't push them along a sales process designed by head office; they'll see it coming and back off. After all, they don't really need you to help them; they can and will do it themselves.

Find their buying process, which usually involves vast amounts of research and checking with their network, stalking the products, checking facts and features, visiting stores, online and brick and then when they're ready, they swoop in for the purchase. Use this buying process and sell alongside it.

They control the buying process; let them keep control and don't take over. Above all, don't use selling techniques with them; they'll see a phoney salesperson very quickly. Perhaps we should get rid of our sales in our titles because they want advisers, helpers, people who can smooth their buying process.

Last week I drove past a new home development which said: "Contact our sales representatives for information". This puts me in fear and dread as a Gen X myself; I want to control and don't want to speak with a sales rep. Urgh.

Let them research. Because they will. They will end up knowing your product better than you. They may even know you better than you know yourself. Help them to educate themselves provide links, sites, online content about you and your service. Videos, White Papers, Blogs. You've heard it all before, but we must do it, as they want to educate themselves before they approach you to close the sale.

However, Gen X's are loyal to a brand once they've done all this research. After all, they don't want to do it again, and once they've proven that the product is right for them and you are trustworthy, they'll stick with you religiously. Brand matters most to Gen X's. Remember, they're trying to be sure about you and your company.

Give them proof. They have cynical sensors built into their heads and will need evidence, cold hard facts about your offering.

No need to build a relationship. I met a Financial Adviser recently who proudly announced to me that he "does business the good old-fashioned way, face to face, and I spend time building a relationship first."

The Adviser was in his mid-60's, and I bet most of his clients were too. Baby Boomer to Boomer this strategy works, but not with Gen X's

This goes against the grain, doesn't it, but it doesn't matter with Gen X's. They're approaching only because they must; they'd rather close the sale online. Don't take it personally, but they've stalked you and your product for a long while; they just want to get the closing over and done with.

No need for chit-chat; get to the point quickly. Take your time with them, have many meetings if you must remember they don't trust you initially. They are reserved with you.

If you've been brought up with relationship building sales practices, don't use them with Gen X's

Involve them. Gen X's want to be in control and learn to trust you. Involve them along the way. Let them see your computer screens, input the details, share the processes you must go through, make the sales process simple, not cumbersome. They don't want to be there longer than expected. Someone tell Head Office, please.

Gen X's foresee problems happening at some time in the future, so present Plan B's in case Plan A goes wrong. Also, give them options and be aware of forcing them down an alleyway. Of course, it's ok to make recommendations, but have a second option up your sleeve. "Based on our discussion, this route would be ideal for you both, but I also have some other ideas if you're interested."

Don't close them. Otherwise, they'll back off. Let them close themselves; they don't want to be shoved into a corner by a pushy salesperson. Invite them to buy, give them space. Ask them if there's any more information they need before you move onwards. Give them thinking time and space to make their own decisions. They will.

Selling to Generation Y

Let's look at how we get to speak with Generation Ys. Self-esteem is critical to them. They don't want to show it with physical trappings of success like their parents, the Boomers; they prefer to be acknowledged by people around them. Ever since they were born, they've been told how special they are, and they have begun to believe it. So, if you're prospecting for their custom, make them feel unique and individual.

Approach them in the reception and literally hold their hands to help them purchase. They've never had to make many decisions in their lives – their parents have done this for them – so allow them to make the decision to talk with you. Provide them with structure and outline the next steps with them. Use signposting regularly.

It goes without saying but use new technology to reach this audience individually. Start referring to social media as Social, and you'll be accepted. They have totally taken this as a way of communicating; it's their way. Embrace it. Think about their world and put your message out to them. Prevent using email – they just don't get it.

So you get to sit them down and talk with them. Generation Ys have short attention spans as they are the most over-scheduled generation, and their friends come before you. Dump the 2-hour interviews. I know it's difficult, but we've got to find a way; otherwise, we won't get this audience. Go beyond 30 minutes, and you've lost them, so break down your interview format. Use technology more before and afterwards to reduce the time spent face to face, and adapt your sale to them. You'll capture a massive market as a result.

Generation Ys strive to be happy. They've delayed responsibility to enjoy themselves more, choosing to have families and mortgages later. They want gap years to travel the world, find themselves, chill-out times, and have "me" times.

Make your product make them feel good about themselves.

Let your product immediately affect them since they're used to instant gratification. Offer them instant solutions as they live in an instantaneous world. Give them the on-the-spot mortgage offer, use lenders that automate the valuation systems, rely on web-based employment checking, arrange for them to get their credit card that day, give them instant decisions by empowering sales staff more. Nothing irritates them more than going to head office for a decision. Remember, they have little loyalty to your company.

Individualise your product, provide customisation, make them feel individual and unique. Ensure your product can be tailored to their needs but don't make the decision too onerous. This will cause stress, and they've never experienced this as their parents shielded them as much as possible.

Highlight any charitable practices you or your company adopt. Focus on ethical funds, have the points from the credit card go to Greenpeace, publish your firm's recycling targets, show them that your firm is an excellent corporate citizen and thinks of others before profits. Use recyclable paper; better still, don't use any paper – make it all electronic so it's quick, instant, and much kinder on the environment.

Be very, very good with your technology. Don't fumble with the laptop keys; you'll get away with this from some generations – boomers and matures will sympathise with you, but Generation Ys won't.

Back To My Shopping Mall

Are the salespeople adapting themselves according to the generations in front of them? Not deliberately, by chance, but relying on luck is not a positive strategy. Use the ideas from this chapter and ensure you connect with all 4 generations at any given time. And has it made my shopping experience any more enjoyable?

Not really, but it's fun watching the lone Gen X customers checking their iPhones for a cheaper product at the till, the matures desperate for someone to connect with them, the Boomers enjoying the selling process and the Gen Ys hovering around in packs checking WhatsApp to see what their friends are saying.

Is the world stereotypical? Yes, it is, at least in a shopping mall.

Social Selling and Lead Generation

The art of using the internet to find, nurture and meet new customers.

Social Selling and Prospecting

Think of inventions before their time. Electric cars were first put on the road in the early 1900s. No mileage there. Video calling from the late 1960s. Didn't connect. Motorised scooters from the late 1800s, no spark there.

These inventions have re-appeared in the last few years and gained traction and popularity. Because they were introduced way before their time.

Social selling was introduced too early and is only now gaining a footing within the financial services advice sector.

The concept of Social Selling has bounced around since around 2007, just before the financial crash. When I mention the phrase to financial and mortgage advisers, most groan, wanting to do the "old school" way of getting new business.

You can understand their view. Old school methods still work, and it's the techniques that many financial advisers are versed in.

These are leaflets, posters, wedding fayres, calling, networking, sponsoring the local football team or the roundabout outside of town, posters, radio advertising, hotel room seminars and presentations, merchandise, hospitality, etc.

What is Social Selling?

Social selling has come of age. Most of our working day is spent online; we're working with clients on video more now since the pandemic. We're chatting to BDMs on video and generally spending many hours glued to a screen of some kind. Even on the train home, we're tethered to our phones online.

So why should we not use online for our prospecting? Maybe it's the phrase "social" that puts people off. Social media is not everyone's cup of tea; I get that. But the whole idea of social selling is merely using the internet to find, nurture and meet new customers.

That's it. Use the internet to find people – they're usually on social media because that's where people "hang out" online. Nurture them, build a relationship and then reach out to meet them in real.

It's not more complicated than that. Let me show you how.

Marketing v Selling

The first realisation essential to accepting social selling is our role as a mortgage or financial adviser. We're not marketers; some of us are lucky to have large departments of marketers who do "marketing". It generates leads for us to contact and sell to.

I've recently worked alongside a mortgage advisory firm with a strong marketing team that generates leads. The advisers pick these leads, phone them, and begin the sales process. Apart from finding out about the customer, where they came from, and their journey so far, the adviser is not involved in the lead generation.

That's the realm of the marketer.

Marketing brings customers to the door – salespeople or advisers then sell or advise the customer; they close the sale.

Broadly that's the difference, but the dilemma facing many solo advisers is they don't have a marketing team, or their firm expects them to market themselves. I call this personal marketing or prospecting. It's not selling; it's attracting customers to your door where you can start selling.

Pipeline Management

That's where pipeline management comes in. Good advisers will have a robust CRM – Customer Relationship Management software – that houses all your customer details.

Customers that enter your CRM for the first time are new customers or prospects. They enter your pipeline, which leads to your sales process.

Blueprint for Pipeline Management

We need some structure, a blueprint maybe. Otherwise, you'll be all over social media trying to drum up some business, and you'll just waste a load of time.

Seriously, social media can be one of the most significant wastes of time on the internet. Look at any teenager glued to their phone during supper.

No, we need to be serious and business-like when using social selling. Here's how.

1.   **Find, prospect potential customers online**

- LinkedIn
- Facebook Ads
- Google Ads
- Google My Business
- YouTube Channel
- Review sites
- Podcasts – guesting or hosting
- Articles on sites
- Your website

2.   **Connect and engage with people online**

3.   **Reach out to people offline e.g.**

- Phone
- Messaging apps
- Email
- Webinar invites
- Video email

4.   **Add to CRM system, continue to reach out**

5.   **Join all "old school" ways of prospecting**

- Personal referrals
- business connection referrals
- paid online leads
- inbound enquiries from website and online presence
- Wedding fayres, leaflet drops, merch etc. etc.

6.   **First stage of adviser/sales process**

There you have it, a robust blueprint to enable you to use social selling to generate leads that will accompany your "old school" methods. Call it hybrid if you like. The word "hybrid" seems to quash most people's opinions; everyone just agrees with a hybrid.

Did you spot the cavernous gap between numbers 2 and 3? Have another look. Yes, that's right, online migrates quickly into offline otherwise, you'll just hide behind the internet and lose hours, days, weeks online getting nowhere.

Some new advisers like to hide behind the internet. They tell you they're prospecting online, but you must reach out to people…offline at some point.

Scary, isn't it.

Personal Branding, Online and Offline

Most social media sites and venues require that you set up a profile. LinkedIn is a great example, and I'll use this for the remainder of the chapter. The concepts work with all social media profiles. Time spent on your profile is fruitful.

Before you crack on populating your profile, you need to be crystal clear about your personal branding. Not your logo; that's just the surface.

But who you are, what you stand for, what your company is about, and why you do what you do? Who do you work with, what value do you provide clients? What problems do you solve for your clients? What goals do you help them achieve?

A CeMAP Bootcamp student contacted me and fixed up a short video coaching session as they had some questions to ask me. I began by briefly introducing myself. "Don't worry about that, Paul", was the response, "I know all about you and what you're about, and I'm a fan".

It was a lovely gesture, but it proved that my internet presence had done the job. People pick up your brand way before they actually meet you and form an opinion of you which will last way beyond the time they actually meet you.

An interesting exercise is to put your full name in the Google search engine and see what comes up. You may share your name with someone more well known, so key in other aspects about you. For example, Paul Archer Speaker Trainer UK mortgage.

Have a look at what the internet is saying about you. Your various social media profiles will appear first. Gauge the brand you're picking up; is it congruent with who you are? Does it show that you are capable, reliable, professional, knowledgeable, human, ethical? These are all ideal brands for mortgage advisers.

If not, time to start on your online presence. If you intend to find people online using social selling, beware that at some juncture, your targeted people will search you too. That might cement your position or jeopardise it

More on Your Brand

Your brand needs to be clear, compelling and appeal to your targeted customer. If you try and appeal to everyone online, you'll just get lost in the sea of advisers and consultants. Know your segment; know your market before you start.

First impressions matter here. Building up a professional online brand; it's taken me over 25 years. Yes, I started my website in 1997, Friends Reunited in 2002, LinkedIn in 2007.

But it can also take seconds to ruin it.

With that in mind, the next stage is to build your profiles, and dozens of sites teach you that. LinkedIn has hundreds of experts who have videos on YouTube teaching you how to do a profile, so I'm not going to repeat what they say.

What I am going to do, though, is test your current LinkedIn profile.

The LinkedIn Social Selling Index – SSI

The SSI is an insightful way of measuring the effectiveness of your profile. It gives you a score, which might shock you or please you. Moreover, it shows you where you can improve your profile and how. Then it re-scores you, and you can measure your improvement.

It's pretty clever, but then LinkedIn is owned by Microsoft, and they're intelligent people who work there. And hungry shareholders who want you to use LinkedIn more and generate advertising revenue for the owners.

So you can see why the information is freely available.

Photofeeler

I just love this site. It allows you to upload your profile photo or two, wait a short while as members of the worldwide public rate your picture. They judge you against:

- Competence
- Likeability
- Influence

Don't take it too seriously; people remain anonymous when they vote for you, tend to go with the immediate first opinion and may not be kind. But it's a good indicator.

Go on, try it.

5 C's to Succeed in Social Selling

- Contact
- Connect
- Consistency
- Creation
- Curation

Contact

When you're clear of your target market, you can start searching for potential customers. Remember, all you're doing is finding people at this stage who may or may not be interested in what you do. Potential customers looking for a mortgage, remortgages, development finance, a business referral partnership, landlords to refinance and so on.

Beware, though; all the other mortgage advisers are doing the same thing, so you'll have to come across as unique and valuable. Therefore you focussed earlier on your personal branding and the value you bring to certain people.

You must be very selective, very picky. Almost qualifying people before you reach out.

Naturally, you can operate inbound online marketing. This relies on your massive internet presence attracting inbound traffic. It works too, but slowly. Your articles attract people, and they might want to connect with you as a valuable source.

Personally, I have lots of "bait" out there on the internet that catches people and lures them onto my CRM system. I have:

- Weekly podcasts to attract listeners on Spotify and Apple
- Videos on YouTube
- Weekly Livestreams on LinkedIn, YouTube and Facebook
- LinkedIn postings two or three times a week
- Articles and writings all over the internet
- Adverts on Facebook and a Facebook Business Page
- Review sites with testimonials being added each week
- A website that has good Google "juice."

All my "bait" has a call-to-action where people can connect with me if they want. It works well for me, but I don't need many new customers to be patient.

Taking the fishing analogy, it's like fishing all day and catching just one fish. But you had a lovely relaxing time sitting and napping by the riverbank in late summer.

How to Find Prospects

Professional fisherman or women go out to sea in a trawler, throw out bait, use sat nav to find shoals and use a giant net to lure in hundreds of fish at a time. They spend two or three days just fishing and nothing else. Cleverly they also throw out unwanted fish or too small examples. In a way, they qualify what they actually want to take back to the harbour and sell.

This parallel works very well.

If you want more new customers, you have to act like a trawler fisherman, not a Sunday afternoon hobbyist. Here are a few ideas to make contact:

- LinkedIn or Sales Navigator search engines. Use these to search for people you may wish to start following, commenting on posts and eventually connecting with. You may want to follow them first, find out more about them, join their groups and then connect.

- Keep your eye on trigger events in your industry. Triggers are events that indicate the person may want to benefit from your services. They can be external or internal. External events happen naturally, such as a new development built near the town or a pandemic that encourages people to vacation at home. Both of these events can mean someone may need your mortgage services. Internal affairs are more insightful. A firm may be expanding and struggle to get the right people or develop into a new business area. These events may trigger the need for your services.

- You can search for triggers by using Google Alerts. This is a free service that you use to key in trigger words or search words. Google then sends alerts to you with links where these search words appear. You then search these and dig around. Jolly useful.

- I love a press release. These are all online now and can tell you what firms are doing and who is involved.

- LinkedIn, Twitter both have trigger event search capabilities, so use them to automate your research.

- LinkedIn Newsfeed will help you find people, but Sales Navigator is definitely recommended. It's a first-class piece of software if LinkedIn is your site of choice.

- # work very well. Search for common #s to find relevant postings

Remember, you're merely finding people at this stage. Please be selective; only find people interested in what you do, don't use the methods to blanket everyone. That just creates animosity and rejection. The secret sauce is to research who you want to find. The narrow this search, the better, the more niche you operate, the more successful you'll be prospecting online.

The next step is to connect.

Connect

This is when you reach out to potential customers to make a connection. Naturally, your inbound efforts may see you getting people connecting with you. Beware, you will be found precisely the same way by salespeople trying to sell you something, so treat this as a learning event but don't accept everyone.

Research them thoroughly and make a connection that is tailored and specific. You can do this by following them, learning about them and their triggers, liking and sharing their posts, and commenting on them. Getting your name in the frame, so to speak.

Finally, send a personal message.

Reaching Out

You must not start selling at this stage. You purely want to connect with them, to help each other. Continue the incubation process, building up trust. But at some point, you need to take them to the first stage of your sales process.

You've done marketing – you've brought them to the front door, now you want to invite them in – offline.

When you're ready, reach out:

- Send a LinkedIn message suggesting a ten-minute call to learn more about them and their needs

- Invite them to an online webinar you're running on the taxation elements of Holiday Buy to Lets.

- Send them some beneficial information to solve their challenges; that's assuming you know what these are. A video explains Holiday Let taxation that you produced, a White Paper, an infographic, a TikTok video, a link to your podcast, a copy of your book.

- Put them on your database emailer, use Mailchimp or the like, to send them regular information.

- Invite them to join your networking group, your Facebook group.

- Email them outside of LinkedIn with a carefully tailored email. Care with this. Email is rarely successful; most are ditched, dumped or ignored by people

Reach out via phone if you have their number. But you better be good at making "cold" calls. They're pretty warm; your customer knows you, so it's not the cold calls that MCOB rules don't like. Again, you have to be polished at these; otherwise, you'll just get voicemail, push back or blatant rejection. Who answers their phone these days anyway?

Internet Adverts

Before I venture onto my last 3 C's of social selling, a quick word around internet advertising. Unless you have a mammoth budget like a bank or national brokerage, you may not be able to secure advertising on the internet to lure potential customers through the door.

I just Googled "Mortgage Affordability Calculator", and the top search results were London and Country, Barclays, Santander and HSBC!

There's a whole book on this topic. Everyone has an opinion about advertising on Google, LinkedIn, Facebook and the like.

For a mortgage adviser, you have a couple of fruitful options, so let me tell you a little more about these:

- LinkedIn events. These allow you to create an audience of people who want to attend your online webinar. Attach this to a site like Eventbrite, and you can quickly automate your next event and drum up potential attendees.

- Lead magnets. Produce a White Paper or report, professional of course, and make it available via a LinkedIn advert. People will leave their contact details in return for the digital item.

- Facebook advertising. This is the number one choice for the solo mortgage adviser. Its enormously cost-effective, highly targeted and reaches consumers. Here's your blueprint:

Facebook Advertising

Facebook. Love 'em or hate them. US politicians seem to have it in for them at the moment, blaming them for everything – stirring racial tensions to encourage anti-vacs.

But whatever you think of them, they're mighty profitable. Last quarter alone, they reported $29 billion in revenue, most of which was from advertising.

The advertising is different to other online platforms. The majority of their customers are small firms, SME's who don't have vast advertising budgets and want to see their advertising targeted and successful. Isn't that the domain of most mortgage broker firms?

Reading this chapter just might inspire you to use them for lead generation. Let me explain to you how.

- Step One – create a Business Page, not your personal page on Facebook, Insta or WhatsApp. This is a professional business page in the same manner as your LinkedIn profile. Populate your profile, pictures, photos etc

- Step Two – start collecting followers, but this might take some time

- Step Three – start posting articles, videos, ideas, house buying tips, new schemes for FTBs etc

- Step Four – choose a post you want to reach more people – perhaps a direct advertising post and then monetise it.

- Step Five - promote it on Facebook and spend £10 or £15. Target your demographic carefully. Choose the geography, age, interests and gender of the people you want to target. For example, you might be promoting equity release to help finance grandchildren's Uni education. Select the postcode GL50 for Cheltenham, select females over 65 who are retired and homeowners. Bingo, Facebook then displays your posting in front of those people; the more you pay, the more people in that group get to see your finely crafted advert. Simple

- Step Six – start putting on online seminars to educate your target audience on equity release. Set it up and promote it on Facebook as an event. Use Eventbrite or another platform to host your webinar and integrate it to Facebook. Promote it in the same way as step five.

Educate, educate, educate once stated Tony Blair. Your clients want to be educated before they see you; no one wants to appear foolish. Online webinars work really well.

Online promotion is the new shopfront for all virtual mortgage brokers, whether you advise face-to-face or virtually. Facebook might just be worth a brief investigation – what have you got to lose - £15?

Consistency

Social selling is akin to flossing your teeth. Flossing has to be done every day before or after brushing. It's a routine to get into since flossing is not the most exciting event that day. But regular flossing brings results. The exact parallel works with tending your garden or looking after pets. Little and often is the answer.

Use this philosophy with social media. Gain traction with the algorithms; they like regular, ongoing connections. Engagement with your followers will place you at the top of the news feed. Regular likes and comments will surge you to the top.

Can you automate this? Many do. A host of automation tools will take the grunt work away from you.

Maybe outsource it to someone in your firm or externally. Many advisers use marketing agencies that do a great job and charge a handsome fee. Perhaps do it yourself. A few minutes spent each day posting and responding on your favourite social sites engaging with would-be customers is time worth spending.

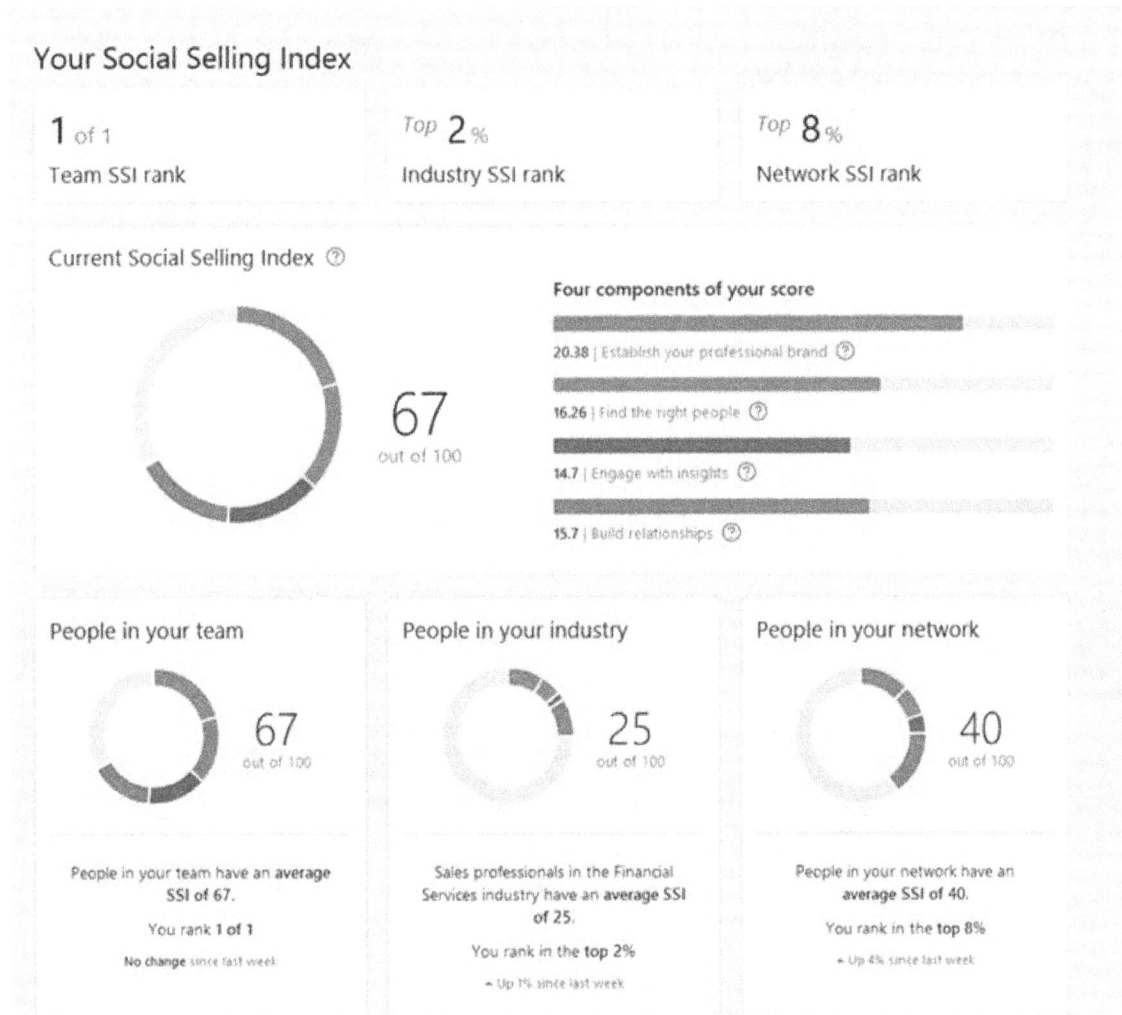

Your Social Selling Index

1 of 1
Team SSI rank

Top **2** %
Industry SSI rank

Top **8** %
Network SSI rank

Current Social Selling Index ⑦

67
out of 100

Four components of your score

20.38 | Establish your professional brand ⑦

16.26 | Find the right people ⑦

14.7 | Engage with insights ⑦

15.7 | Build relationships ⑦

People in your team

67
out of 100

People in your team have an average SSI of 67.

You rank **1 of 1**

No change since last week

People in your industry

25
out of 100

Sales professionals in the Financial Services industry have an **average SSI of 25.**

You rank in the top 2%

↑ Up 1% since last week

People in your network

40
out of 100

People in your network have an average SSI of 40.

You rank in the top 8%

↑ Up 4% since last week

Your LinkedIn SSI will climb if you get involved and get engaged.

I'm a big KPI guy. All of my business activity has a KPI attached to them. My KPIs are one new posting a week on Linked In, one on Facebook Business Page, 3 videos onto YouTube, publishing 3 blog posts weekly and writing 2,500 words each week.

The last KPI takes me onto the next "C" – Creation.

Creation

To post on LinkedIn and other social media sites, you need to write exciting and compelling content. All the usual culprits are acceptable. Photos of meetings, team get-togethers, Award Dinner tables, you with your family, some pithy quotes…are all great.

But the real test is original content that you personally have written or recorded. Suppose you want to get over your knowledge, ability, and professionalism. In that case, you need to move beyond a photo of your cat sleeping on your keyboard. Although being human is essential, it's not all you want to show.

LinkedIn especially likes original content:

- Videos

- Articles – short or long

- Infographics

- Memes

Create content that solves the problems that your targeted customers have. For example, I talk about training and speaking virtually, write articles on this topic, record videos and audios and generally explain how to do it.

My potential coach and training customers can read this, learn how to do it and maybe connect with me as an authority in the venture. Then you go on to connect and engage offline.

You may want to write and record media on mortgages, buying and selling, landlord issues, how to rent holiday lets, Stamp Duty, the housing market, economic issues and so on. Remember to niche as much as you can. Generic information is freely available and quickly found. Tips for First Time Buyers can reveal thousands of identical posts.

Are You Adding to the White Noise?

Attend any social selling or "how to gain guaranteed leads" type of training course, and they'll tell you to create content and educate your potential customers. Informing them of everything you know so they'll find this when searching online, pop along to your website, and do business with you.

The problem is you're just adding to the terabytes of white noise already on the internet freely available on precisely the same subject.

I've seen mortgage advisers post on LinkedIn:

- How to remortgage

- The difference between fixed and variable rates

- The process of buying a house

They're delivered well, some of them. Most are just head and shoulders talking. Now I'm not criticising them; they're doing personal content marketing, which seems like a great way to do it. Still, you're just adding to the already crowded internet of this content.

People now look for interpreters rather than information givers, and there's a huge difference. A giver just gives generic information. An interpreter figures out what you need to know and how to apply it to your current challenges.

Let me give you an example.

Earlier this year, a corporate firm contacted me because they wanted some help closing and getting more customers to commit to their mortgage advisers.

The advisers were not gaining commitment or closing. Many expect their advice to be compelling enough for the customer to accept it without question. There are now many other places they can get the same advice from. So I gave my client ideas on how they could do this in their tightly niched bridging and seconds marketplace with their advisers all based at home.

Do you see, I acted as an interpreter, not an information giver? I tailored the ideas to the industry, in their sector for their problems.

The message is that you want to use this technique as part of your personal marketing strategy to give information and think of your target market and tailor the information. Become an interpreter of the readily available information and make it relevant and unique to your clients.

And please tell me you are targeting a market, aren't you? You're not marketing to everyone on LinkedIn, are you?

Curation

The opposite of creation is curation, which also helps with your postings.

Think of the librarian of old. She could find your books on any subject, so learn to re-share a helpful post from others. Add your "two penneth worth" and send it out to your followers.

Use marketing tools to find content. Search Twitter, Google Alerts, RSS feeds from blogs that you frequent, subscribe to newsletters from industry sources, online newspapers and so on.

Use this method to add variety to your posting. I firmly believe you must be original to create the right brand.

Summary and Call to Action

Is Social Selling and Prospecting an invention before its time? It probably was back in 2007, but I really feel it has found its place for this decade.

We spend almost 100% of our business lives online now; many use online video to conduct our meetings with clients.

So why can't we use the internet to find people that might be interesting? After all, online dating is prevalent. Depending on which statistic you believe in, it's been reported that over 30% of married couples met online.

Incubate, Sell, Repeat

It's Like Distilling Brandy

I've always been rather partial to a cheeky drop of brandy or Cognac, so I was thrilled when my father emigrated to France and bought a tiny fisherman's cottage near Cognac in the heart of France.

That's where they make the stuff, and they're so proud of their process, you can book tours around the breweries to figure out how it works.

Naturally, this was the first thing I did on visiting my father's house.

And it was fascinating but boiled down to 3 factors that directly correlate to prospecting for the busy professional adviser.

- Firstly, they distil the wine, turning the liquid into vapour before returning to liquid entirely distilled.

- Secondly, they do this twice to enhance the flavour.

- Thirdly, it takes an absolute age to complete the process.

I'll show you how this relates.

The Prospecting Engine

So let me share with you the prospecting engine that will ensure you never run out of new business for your professional advisory role. This engine works whatever knowledge you sell. Financial, legal, insurance, management, sales, architectural, accountancy...it doesn't matter so long as you sell your expertise to solve client problems.

The engine works expertly without taking up unnecessary time, but you need to invest one day a week in it. No more and no less; otherwise, you won't be doing much client business. The good news is that once you start it, much of the operation becomes automatic, so it's operational even when you are with clients, whilst you sleep and on vacation.

It doesn't involve hard sell, although you mustn't forget to sell. Many professionals get lured into the content marketing dream because they're reticent to sell. Selling is merely closing, and you have to level with yourself what you are selling to new clients.

If you don't have a rock-solid belief in the value you bring to clients, then the engine won't work since you'll be selling something you don't believe in. This mindset is essential, especially with referral management and making appointment calls.

The Last Century Way To Prospect

Back in the day, and I'm talking the 1980s when I started out in financial advisory sales, we had this concept called the sales funnel. Throw prospects into the top of the funnel en masse, and gradually you would filter them down by qualifying. You'd end up with motivated clients. It was exhausting and involved lots of cold calling and knocking on doors. Marketing departments would advertise for you, putting a large clump of new prospects into the funnel. It was essentially a sales-driven activity.

But the world has changed. We know that, and the facts don't need discussing here. What is clear is that your prospective new clients are in control now and determine the pace of your prospecting.

So we turn the funnel upside down to attract prospects when they want to come in, usually in dribs and drabs rather than en masse. Hence the narrow spout at the top only allows people in one at a time. I'll talk about what to do once they're in, in a moment, but for now, let's focus on how to get prospects to enter your funnel at the narrow end.

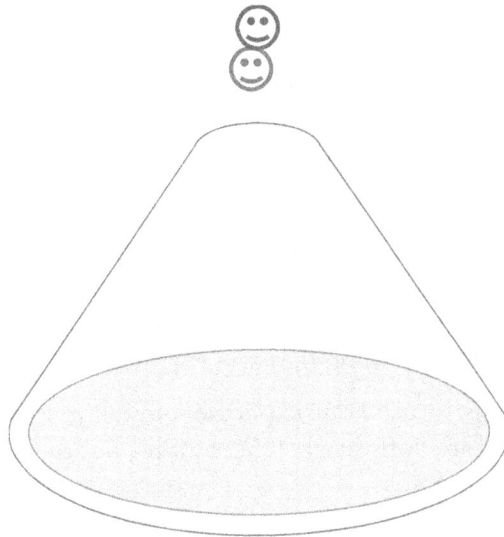

How They Get Into Your Incubator

You can't force them in; they must enter voluntarily, so they need a compelling reason to come and join your incubator. And the reason is they want some of your expertise and wish to hang around with you. So you promise this if they enter.

The most traditional route is via a website sign up form. Your prospect provides you with their name and email address in return for your expertise. And they're in. Many professionals will store these people in some form of auto-responder email programme from the likes of Mailchimp. These firms make it easy to email your expertise regularly, but they don't allow everyone in. Just people who have opted in. You see, they're paranoid about people accusing them of sending out spam, so only let people onto the list who have asked to be there.

Think GDPR.

If you think about it, these people want your expertise and may, one day, buy something from you. But that comes much later; right now, we're merely incubating them.

You can manually add people to your upside-down funnel from various sources. Harvested business cards, previous clients, audiences who have given you their names, your LinkedIn connections, product buyers, Twitter followers, Facebook friends.

The differentiator is that they are only browsing. They don't want to talk to you or buy your expertise; they're just interested in it and are pretty happy to consume the free stuff you provide. One day they might be ready to purchase from you, possibly never. I've had prospects in my upside-down funnel for over 15 years; some of them have never bought anything but love to consume my expertise. You might be one of them.

Keeping Your Incubator Warm

Over time, your incubator will fill with people interested in what you do, so now you have to give them what they want – your expertise. We talked about this in the previous chapter.

Because you are an expert, a professional who sells expertise, you just create content that your audiences want to consume in ways that suit them.

Create content that solves their pains and problems, answers questions your audiences might have, helps them achieve their goals, inspires them, and entertain them. Produce material that clearly demonstrates your expertise. Don't hold back; give them everything; after all, the internet can and does provide everything they will ever need.

Your role, or it should be, is to use your expertise and tailor solutions to individual clients. The materials they consume are "off the shelf" solutions, not the bespoke application of your expertise that you charge a fee for.

Just feed everyone in your incubator with regular, multi-sensory, compelling content.

You're Not Selling, You're Incubating

Why can't I sell to the people in my incubator? After all, I need to make a living? I hear you cry. Of course, you can, and many experts do, sprinkling their posts with adverts and calls to action. My view on this is that you will put more people off than attract clients. Remember, they are in charge, not you, it's their buying process that we want to latch onto, and when they're ready, they'll slip through and reach out.

And that's the next step. Have a look at the diagram, and you'll see our incubator keeps people hovering. Still, they can drop below into the more traditional sales funnel when they want to. There's also a side-entrance if you look closely, which I'll explain.

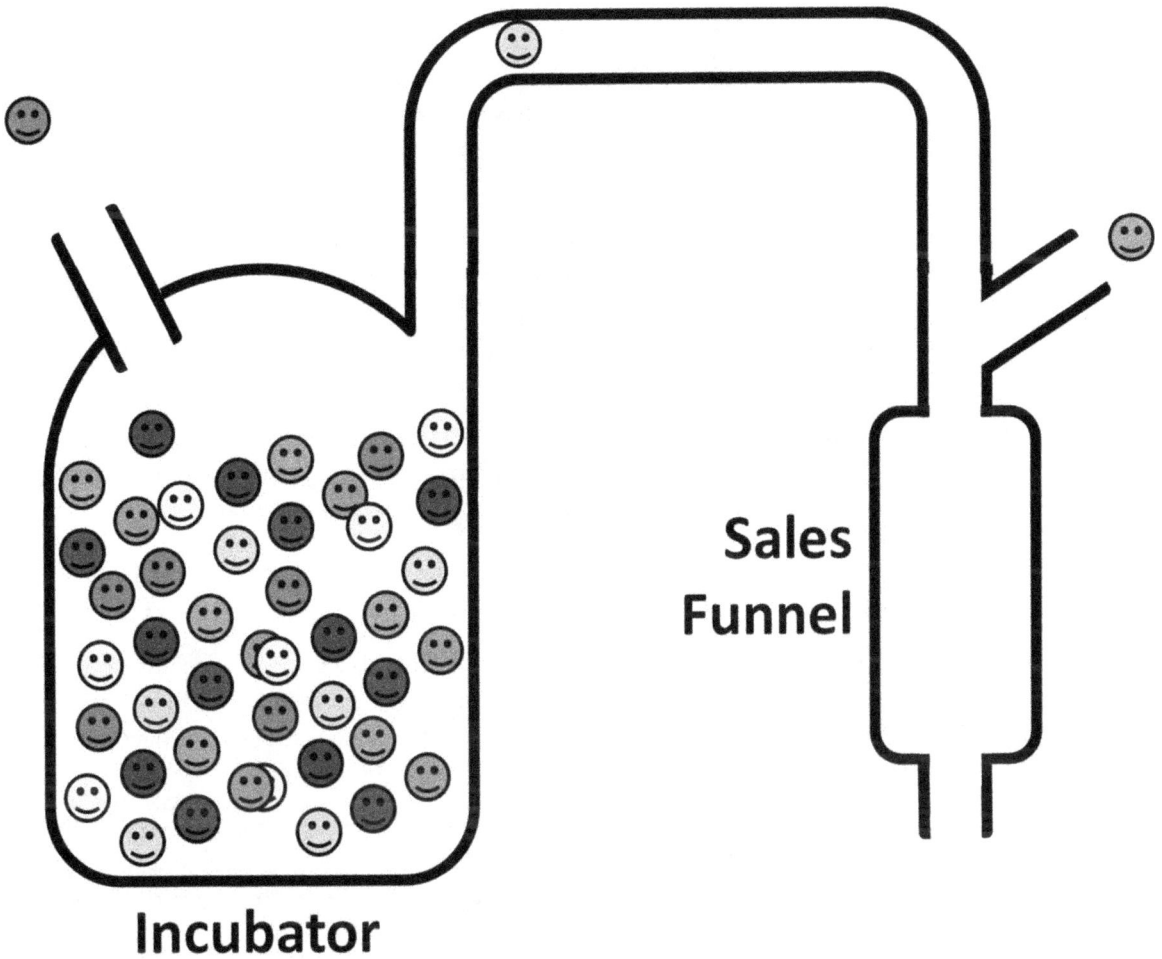

Sales Funnel

Incubator

From Incubator to The Sales Funnel

So far, we've been talking about gradually filling up your incubator over time using expertise in the form of content to lure them in. Over time, they'll come to see you as the person who can solve their needs, so they'll drop out of the incubator into your sales funnel, and this is where the fun starts. Unfortunately, this is the bit many professional advisers forget or leave out of their marketing. Many of us have forgotten to sell as we've been rendered drunk by the lore of content marketing which doesn't have any rejection. The sales funnel we're about to explore has rejection in it...lots.

Take The Side Entrance

This is where you manually enter "hot" prospects to receive the intense treatment. These people are ready to buy, need their pain solved, have a budget to pay for it and may already have heard about you. Those dropping out of the incubator already know you're the "go-to" person; the side entrance is for new entrants.

For me, it's referred prospects either from my client base or my network of friends/colleagues. About 50% of my new business comes from this source, and once they're provided to me, I have to act quickly. Other people here might be those who directly contacted you – phone, email, tweet, text – they found you on the web and need to talk to you quickly.

It could be a bought lead that you've purchased. My accountant secured my business in this way. I reached out to an accountancy forum for local accountants a couple of years ago. The forum charged local accountants to contact me. He paid them, contacted me, and the rest is history.

Your Selling Process

From now on, for a salesperson like me, it gets exciting because you're doing a deal. Prospects that fall into the traditional funnel need special attention. You have incubated candidates who know you, like you, trust you since they've been subjected to your online content expertise for a while, sometimes years.

You have LinkedIn requests from potential clients you've scoped out and realise they have a need you can help with; you have referred prospects looking for you to solve a problem or pain they have. You also have opportunities who have reached out to you pro-actively, so they have a need that desires solving.

You have to activate these; don't expect the sale to drop in your lap; you need to make contact some way and move them along your selling steps, as we used to call our sales process.

Incubate...sell....repeat.

Back To Brandy

And to my brandy analogy. Remember they distil the wine, turning it into vapour before returning to liquid entirely distilled as brandy. And it takes an age to complete, but the end result is pure gold.

Your incubator can keep someone warm for months, even years. It can take an age for the prospect to filter through, but when they do and drop into the sales process part of the funnel, it can turn into gold for you.

After all this hard work, I think I need a brandy!

The Definitive Guide to Referrals for Advisers

Appointment by Referral Only

Bernie Madoff had written on his business card "Appointment by Referral Only", and I've known many Independent Financial Advisers to have this embossed in gold on theirs. Now I'm not condoning Bernie; of course, he's a crook, but the impact of exclusively building your business from referrals and introductions from clients is Nirvana for professional advisers.

I love referrals in my business, which is professional advising like yours. It ticks all the boxes. A 90% closing ratio, they follow your recommendations without hesitation, it has a meagre cost of sale enabling superior client service, removes risk from the client's perspective, there's little or no competition. You're able to reciprocate to your clients in the form of recommendations for their business.

Who Wouldn't Want Referrals?

Far too many of us operate the "Pray and Wait" methodology. I've met many an adviser who has been in business for over 25 years and received organic referrals regularly. And why wouldn't they? 25 years of servicing clients, and you'll be blessed with organic referrals; in other words, clients make referrals on their own initiative. It's not a managed service.

Suppose you're looking to expand your business and increase your client bank, or you're new to an area or industry. In that case, adopting a referral management system is a must. And I'm going to show you how to use my own "Stepping Stones ©" technique, which will bring you substantial success.

Like all business model changes, you have to believe in it. I've trained hundreds of professional services people who agree wholeheartedly with the concept of referrals. Still, when it comes to asking clients, they shy away. "Too pushy, too salesey, it feels awkward, they'll refer if they want to" are just some responses.

Let's eradicate this Inner Game thinking first.

Belief Systems for Referrals

Do you have an abundance mindset, a belief of feast? This is where you believe wholeheartedly in what you do and the immense value to clients. You offer a superior service, do a great job, and indeed are an expert in your field. This self-confidence comes with time, don't wait to receive validation from external sources or feedback…you are valid.

The acid test is this. If you were in the market for the professional service you provide, you would buy from you, wouldn't you?

My research and work in professional services fire up the following beliefs that support an abundance mindset:

1. I'm responsible for the outcomes of my role

2. I'm good at solving client problems and issues

3. I feel good about myself and my abilities

4. I have rugged self-esteem

5. I'm an expert in my niche

6. I'm clear on the value that I bring to the table

7. I want to build my clients' businesses and be regarded as a trusted partner

8. I'm here to build long-term relationships with clients

9. I know I can add value to clients

10. I know what I want

11. Even if I don't make any sales, I'll feel good about my performance

12. Change is good

13. I compare very favourably with other professional services people

14. I am confident in what I do

15. I believe in the bigger picture rather than the detail

16. Stepping outside my comfort zone is scary but vital for my self-development

17. I am capable of keeping abreast of all industry problems and challenges

18. I believe in sometimes asking really tough questions and enjoying the silence

19. Everything I do adds value to clients

20. I wholeheartedly believe that to grow my business, I can achieve this exclusively with a proactive referral management system

The last belief is the cornerstone to being successful with referrals. If you feel you want and need to adopt this belief and own it, then here's a little bit of Neuro-Linguistic Programming (NLP) to help. It's about questioning away from the belief first.

Write down below your current belief around adopting and succeeding in a proactive referral system. Go on and be honest.

Now ask yourself these questions or, better still, get a colleague to do so. Verbalise the answers, don't dwell on them too long; answer all the questions within 5 minutes. Be honest with the answers.

1. What is your limiting belief?

2. Does this belief help you?

3. What examples can you think of when your limiting belief was inaccurate or didn't apply?

4. How is this belief ridiculous?

5. What caused you to have this belief in the first place?

6. What's the consequence of having this belief?

7. If you keep this belief, what will it cost you in the future?

8. For whom is this belief not true?

9. Do top-performing professional advisers have this belief?

10. How would you know if this belief were false?

11. What was the original purpose for having this belief?

12. What do you want to believe in instead?

13. What would be the advantage to you of having this new belief?

Now we have the right mindset, we need the appropriate context for setting up a referral management system. Professional advisers who have this nailed regard clients as partners. I like that – it's equal and smells of reciprocity – if they help you, you can help them with referrals. After all, you are partners now. It's a nice touch when you begin to refer to them as a partner at the end of the first dealings with your client.

The Context for a Referral Management System

To conquer the "needy" mindset, advisers set a context of scarcity. They're not desperate for new business; they are proactively expanding their client bank but only allowing one or two more clients in.

I admire the scarcity mentality, which increases desire – Cialdini's influencing strategies – a classic. Expanding the business entails heavy marketing spend and time, which takes them away from servicing clients.

Referrals are a meagre, almost nil cost of sale, and reward the client by knowing that the people they refer can have access to you. Access which they've enjoyed and had tremendous value from. This context-setting happens early on; it's logical, compelling, and ultimately successful.

Paul's Referral Management Aphorisms

1. Clients should know how they benefit from being partners and helping with referrals.

2. Clients should be crystal clear of the type of clients you help best. Does anyone know anyone called "anybody", so why ask them for anybody?

3. Clients should be aware of all the value you provide, not just the segment of your expertise that they've benefitted from.

4. Clients should know exactly what you'll do when they lay on a referral. Use the "non-sales, just an exploratory approach". They don't want you to steam in and force a sale on their referral. This is one of the most significant hurdles in the client's mind that prevents from them offering a name. "I'll fix up an exploratory meeting on my dollar, no pressure, see if there's some synergy, and I'll give feedback to you. They'll be in good hands."

5. Be pure in your intentions.

With the principles over, let's begin the Stepping Stones©

Stepping Stones© Referral Management System

A small river blocks my way to my local pub, the Red Lion, called the River Chelt. When the water levels are low, there's one place you can cross. It comprises 3 stepping stones and ensures a dry crossing every time. You're virtually guaranteed to get an early bath if you try and jump the river.

This analogy works in the world of referrals.

However, many of us are reticent to ask customers, putting us off by saying they'll have a think about it. You see, it's too much to ask all of a sudden; it's like jumping the river, you'll fall in.

Instead, adopt a Stepping Stones method.

Let me give you an example. A few years ago, I bought a small gadget that attaches itself to my broadband router and feeds extra Wi-Fi from my phone when I need it most. It's boosted my speed by 3 times, pretty cool.

I "live chatted" as I had several questions to ask. I said thank you for their help, and the chap typed back; it was a pleasure to help with any query as they valued customer service since most of their new business comes from referrals.

Seed is sown and the first Stepping Stone.

Next is the installation, where you "live chat" with them again as it installs. It worked perfectly, and the chap typed in, "If you're pleased with the service and results, would you be so kind as to give us a review on Trust Pilot." I was pleased, so I did.

Feedback is given and Stepping Stone number two.

Finally, a follow-up email came in asking if it was working well. I replied yes, and the following email offered me a voucher to refer two friends to them. I did.

Stepping Stone number three and success.

If they had just waited until the end to ask, I doubt if they would have been successful. They also used reciprocity to make me owe them a favour. Clever.

It really does work, too and eats very little of your phone's expensive data. Thank you, Boosty.

My two dogs ignore the stepping stones over the River Chelt; they love to cool down in the cold waters.

Step One - Sowing the Seed

Janine is in her client's office, he's the CEO of a local firm, and he's contacted Janine to discuss loan finance for the expansion plans he has for his business. The meeting went well, and Janine had further discussions with their firm's accountants.

Janine - "Brian, I think this has been a fruitful first meeting, don't you think?"

Brian - "Yes, interesting, and I'm keen to explore further what you can do. Let me know how you get on with Shelley."

Janine - "Of course, I will. Before I leave, though, can I say it's been a pleasure, I believe I was referred to you by a colleague, and that's an excellent way to do business. Here at Jupiter, we focus on client referrals rather than spending time and money on marketing efforts, preferring to be very competitive with our lending. We're going through some extensive expansion plans just like you, and we've decided to focus on referrals to build our client base. That way, Brian, I can spend all my time with you and my other clients."

Brian - "That makes total sense."

Janine - "So when we get to the 'I'm impressed stage', you might feel comfortable to look through your network to see who might benefit in the same way as you have. But we'll wait until then because I've got to concentrate on impressing you first."

Brian - "Janine, that's excellent; great to meet you today."

Janine - "Same, shall we LinkIn in the meantime? I'll send you a LinkedIn request later if that's OK."

Brian - "Splendid."

Seed sown

Step Two - Value Discussion

Back in the late summer of 2016, we had some friends over for a couple of days. The morning of the night before, we all sat around having breakfast at the local pub, the Red lion, of course, and the discussion turned to the Olympics. As you know, the Brits did well, coming second in the medals table to the mighty USA. We shared some personal memories of the games while chewing on our sausages and celebrated together with the bacon.

We wallowed in the success of the Brits. And that's the value discussion. It's a short agenda item where you ask the client about her value; what outcomes has she achieved with your advice, what has the value been like? It's all about timing and having the value discussion when the client has first-hand experienced the value you provide.

Email calendar invites from Janine:

- Agree on next stages

- Value discussion

Janine - "Last item on our agenda Brian, the value discussion. I'm interested in what value you've gained from our work together at this stage. Do you mind me asking?"

Brian - "Ummmm, interesting question. On the results-driven piece, you've met my demands for the lending proposition. I really valued the way you explored our business here and your time with the team, especially Shelley and her team. You're competitive, which is vital for the targets to fit, and I'm looking forward to this continuing. All in all, Janine, I'd say you've delivered for us."

Janine - "That's great to hear. Has there been anything you weren't expecting and valued?"

Brian - "I have a saying here at Acal; 'over promise and over deliver' rather than the under-promise version, we like to give our customers a delightful experience. Hand on heart, Janine, I think you're achieving that which is why we agreed to do the business with you."

Janine - "Wow, I've not heard the 'over-promise and over-deliver" phrase, nice. Brian, can you remember earlier when you sought some references for the bank and me? You were keen to eliminate risk at that early stage, weren't you? Could I call upon you for a reference that I can use with future clients that would be so helpful?"

Brian - "I'd be delighted. Do you have a template I could use to save time?"

Janine - "Yes, I can email it over to you. You can edit it if you wish; it's just a start to save you time. And if you could put it on headed paper, I'd be grateful."

Brian - "Leave it to me. If you email it to Penny and give her those instructions, I'll sign the bottom."

Janine - "Thank you, and I look forward to meeting again next week when we finalise everything."

References, testimonials, and net promoter scores come in various guises nowadays. Still, the value of a third party endorsing what you do is immeasurable. Testimonials can go on LinkedIn, Unbiased.com, vouchedfor.com, trustpilot.com.

Step Three – The Introduction

Janine - "Well, Brian, that about wraps up the details; if you can get the FD to countersign, we're good to go."

Brian - "Excellent."

Janine - "Brian, do you remember a short while ago when we first met, I mentioned that Jupiter is going through an expansion phase and ensuring our products remain competitive and our service personal, we've decided to grow with partner referrals?"

Brian - "Yes, I do; I was particularly impressed with your strategy; it made sense to me."

Janine - "As a business partner, which I refer to you as I'd like to talk to you about that right now because your name would add a lot of weight. Is that OK? It'll take around 10 minutes?"

Brian - "Shoot."

Janine - "My specialist field is electronics which is why I'm working with you; I find it easy to understand the sector with my experience. I've a list of various firms from this sector in this area; I've been conscious to ensure they're not competitors with you. I was wondering whether you had connections in these firms you could introduce me to?"

"Before you answer that, Brian, let me outline what I would do if you were able to refer a connection to me. With all referrals, I offer them a pure exploratory meeting on my dollar, no pressure; I'm not going to sell anything, just show them the kind of value that I provided you. I believe in synergy; if it's not there, we'll say our farewells and move on. How does that sound to you, Brian? "

Brian - "I'd have expected that, but it's reassuring to know. Let me have a look at your list….uhmm…no, no…yes, I know Philip at Zynga, he's in Round Table with me, I'd be delighted to make a referral."

Janine - "Thank you, Brian, there are a few more companies on the next page…."

Many professional advisers make the grave mistake of asking for anyone you know; this is an error. No one knows a person named anybody. It's wrong in two areas: One, it often leads the client to put you off, saying they'll think about it later, and to avoid any conflict, advisers move on from this. Secondly, it doesn't help you because you know your ideal client, your sector, or your niche and spending valuable time on an "anybody" is not a good use of your time.

Has anyone ever heard of someone called "anybody"? It's ridiculous.

Other strategies that work at the introduction stage:

- Use the LinkedIn connections from your client. You would have linked in at an early stage, so take a look at their relationships and pick out specific people you would like an introduction to. This can be done face to face with your client in a similar manner to Janine's meeting, or you can use the LinkedIn engine to automate the referral.

- Talk about the client's own business. Other departments, subsidiaries or their supply chain. That's bound to jog their memory.

- Make the client feel ok with this by suggesting: "To jog your memory Mike, here's a list of my ideal types of clients."

- Reciprocate. Offer to provide the client with a referral from your network. Now they're a true partner.

- And above all, remember to maintain control of the referral management, don't leave anything to chance.

Janine - "Thank you, Brian. Let's summarise the next steps. You've agreed to phone Philip to expect my call; I'll do that and fix up an exploratory meeting to see if I might help with his plans, and I'll let you know how I get on."

When Brian phones Phil:

Brian - "Phil, it's Brian; no, it's not about Saturday's paintball. I've given your name to Janine White from Jupiter, she's the best loans adviser I've ever come across, and I know you're looking to expand in China. She'll give you a call, make sure you do everything she says, follow all her advice and pay her whatever her fee is. You won't be disappointed. Now Saturday…."

Referral Nirvana.

Handling "Push-Back"

My son started university back in 2017. We were all super excited until we heard the news about a meningitis issue on campus. All students are offered a free vaccine; of course, Euan had his before leaving.

More recently, we've been rescued from disaster with a vaccine programme that's one of the best in the world. This has relieved the COVID nightmare.

It's all about prevention rather than a cure, and that's the way professional advisers should deal with concerns and push back from clients. We're not in the mould of 1990s direct salespeople who are still taught objection handling techniques.

No, we pre-empt instead by building vaccines into our process, demonstrating our professionalism and expertise.

If we take the push back you might receive when asking for referrals, typically I hear professional advisers tell me their clients say:

- "I'll have to think about it."

- "I'll call you when I think of someone."

- "I don't know anyone."

- "I'm tied up at the moment."

These responses are widespread when the professional adviser storms in at the end with the ubiquitous "Do you know anybody?" Remember, no one was ever given the name Anybody.

However, when you use the Stepping Stones© methodology, you're naturally pre-empting each of these.

That's being professional. So if you use this approach, you shouldn't have clients respond as above.

If you hit a brick wall, treat them as knee jerk reactions.

I remember being fascinated as a child when the doctor would tap your leg just below the knee on the patellar tendon, causing a reflex action. We know this as the knee jerk reaction, and it's more commonly attributed to an immediate emotional, unthinking response produced by an event or statement to which the reacting person is compassionate.

Your client is probably stressed in some way, probably thinking of their next meeting or their emails piling up and isn't giving your question the time it needs to process.

The response you'll get is:

- "I can't think of anyone."

- "I don't know anyone on the list."

In these situations, we acknowledge heavily with an "I understand", or "I fully appreciate that", or "that's fine", but we must immediately respond just to take them out of their reflex action. Some of my favourites are:

- "If you can refer someone you know, there's not going to be any sales pressure at all, just an exploratory meeting to begin with."

- "We're connected on LinkedIn. Would you mind if I took a glance at your connections to see if there is someone on there you'd be able to refer?"

- "Let's say hypothetically that we swapped jobs today. Out of interest, who would be the first three people you would call to generate business?"

- "If you had a housewarming party, who would be the first 3 people you invite?"

And as for my son Euan, the last thing he's worried about when going to Uni is meningitis; he was about to experience the most incredible adventure of his life. Lucky lad.

Fixing Appointments from Leads

It's January, and the mass hordes are flocking to the gyms to work off the pounds from Christmas and fulfil their New Years' Resolutions. We all know many would have given up by February but will still be paying that direct debit gym membership.

We've all been there.

Paying good money for no return.

The parallel extends to bought mortgage leads from a marketing agency or an internet company. You often pay substantial amounts for a lead, but you turn these into appointments. This chapter will show you how to maximise your investment and achieve more face-to-face meetings, which you can turn into income.

The Process:

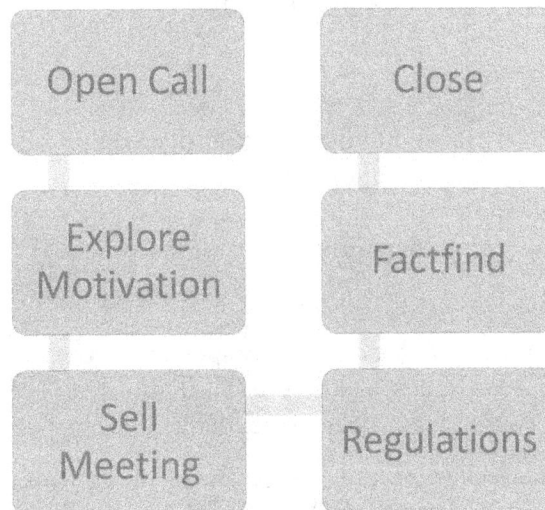

Open

You must aim to call the lead as soon as received; delay, and you'll lose the impact. Even if it arrived at night, try and at least text that you'll phone in the morning.

"Hi, I'm Paul from ABC, we mortgage specialists. You were online just now and wanted to speak with someone about a mortgage."

"The reason for my call is to see what we can do to help you, and if it's a good time, I'd like to find out what it is you want to achieve?"

Note, I don't use the "is it convenient?", which never works.

"is that OK?"

Use plenty of test closes to get the customer nodding and agreeing. Yes-tags work well here as well, don't they?

Explore

This is what we all do well as mortgage advisers. The capability to ask questions. You're not fact-finding though, you're exploring the motivation behind the call, seeking the customer's hot buttons. More than likely, they were online doing the ubiquitous research. They reached a point where they couldn't research anymore and needed further help.

Are they looking to consolidate some loans? Are they re-mortgaging? Have they had trouble obtaining mainstream finance? Seek their motivation to contact someone.

Use plenty of verbal assertions and paraphrase. Enable them to talk.

Summarise when they've finished and confirm the meeting.

Sell the Meeting

"We've helped hundreds of people in your position over the last 5 years and are experts in this area. I could ask you some more questions, then fix up a meeting with you. We can then discuss some options and show you some new ideas that'll help you to bring all your loans together under one highly competitive mortgage."

"How does that sound?"

Remember to test close and don't come across desperate for the business; note the "I might be able to" much softer. Customers also like to hear the word "options and ideas". They seriously don't want to receive advice; believe me, that's regulator speak, not customer speak.

At this junction, you may feel some push-back. Be ready for this. Typically, you'll get the "send me some literature". You need to deal with these, so plan your responses. I like to work with the principle of knee jerk reactions. Think about it. When we are pushed for a decision, we all react instantly with a "no" – we knee jerk react. It's built into our DNA.

So, when faced with a typical "I'm not sure" or a "send me literature", merely re-ask what it is you asked for. Make sure you acknowledge what they've just said and just state the same request you made earlier. They've now had time to think about it and will be positive.

Regulations and Fee

You've got to do this; otherwise, you'll have your compliance people down on you like a ton of bricks but do it customer-friendly, don't use regulator speak.

"Have you heard of the Financial Conduct Authority?"

"They look after us to ensure you get sound advice from us, and we're directly regulated with them. That means we can give you access to every bank, building society and lender, many you've never heard of, can't find on the internet and are only able to deal through me."

Now drop a landmine if the customer is inclined to talk to someone else.

"You see, if you went direct to your bank, they could only give you options from within their products and many people online also have restricted options; I can look at all the lenders for you."

"Does that sound interesting?" Note another test close. Now comes the crucial part.

"You might be wondering how I earn a living. First, if we meet up, there's no charge at all for that meeting, and if we can help you, we'll arrange everything, sort out all the online paperwork and forms, talk to all the people we need to. We do that all for you and charge a fee, but I can let you know exactly how much that will be when we meet, and you can normally add it to the loan so you won't have to fork out for it upfront."

Here you may get push back again. Handle it. Re-assert you'll talk through the amount when you meet. If you need to, you can alleviate by announcing it'll be less than £500, but this is dangerous as the customer might start wanting more detail. State that the first meeting is on your dollar, so there's no harm talking.

Factfind

The pure purpose of the next series of questions is to qualify the customer, not fact-finding. You don't want to go see everyone; you need to check to see that you can help; it's the type of customer you usually work with; they're not going to shop around outrageously. They are the type of customer where a fee is relatively standard.

"I want to make sure we can help you."

Close

Confirm you can help and fix the meeting.

"Great news, I'm confident I can help you, so you don't need to go anywhere else. Shall we fix up a time to talk further?"

Follow this methodology, and you'll be successful with most leads. You won't have that guilty feeling of paying the gym membership every month and avoiding any benefit. But you still might have those extra few pounds on you from Christmas – I know, I have.

Handling the Competition with Bought Internet Leads

Chapter Summary

Paul introduces you to advisers' challenges when selling to leads bought on the internet. They are pricy but targeted and quick to turn around. But you can "burn" them very quickly – known as "burning your data."

Enough to bring a shiver from any sales director.

Paul lays down how to avoid the challenges with some straightforward selling techniques whilst remaining competent and compliant.

A Burning Problem

One of the hottest methods of gaining leads in the mortgage sector is via the internet. These leads cost money, and the biggest problem is that they are dead easy to "burn". A disaster since they can be highly successful methods of building your client bank and achieving your business goals with a bit of training.

I've recently worked with several clients selling loans and financial products in a regulated advisory capacity. They're doing so remotely, from home. Their leads come from the internet, arriving as text messages or "data" that needs responding to as soon as possible.

Internet Leads

My clients advise (sell) income protection, travel insurance, private medical insurance, second charge loans (homeowner loans) and bridging loans. You also have the usual culprits of first charge mortgages for various uses and life assurance, building insurance and ancillary products like wills and Lasting Power of Attorney (LPA).

The whole gamut, you would say.

The common denominator is that their leads arrive from the internet, not from traditional marketing if there ever is such a thing nowadays.

These leads cost them money, data is expensive, and burning it unnecessarily costs too much. So their skills in handling the leads need to be top-drawer, and they need to accept that although they are regulated mortgage or insurance advisers, they have to follow sales steps to achieve success.

This mindset change or belief is hard to stomach sometimes. Just because you have passed your exams and achieved CAS doesn't mean that every customer will buy your advice; that's naive.

Let me share what I've learned and coached with my customers over the years, particularly now, in the pandemic and the new economy.

The Customer's Buying Process

The first technique is to adopt or live the customer's process before arriving at your door. When you buy leads from the internet using aggregators, websites or Google ads, people would have been on their buying spree online and solo.

They would have progressed their buying process online. Many would be far along with the steps they usually follow when buying something. Everyone has a buying process, and they stick to this more rigidly when purchasing big-ticket items or purchases that need a careful decision, such as loans or mortgages.

The first step for you is to agree with this. Just know that they will be 50% to 70% along their process, and you need to find out where they are speedily.

Otherwise, they will take over and ask you questions, which new advisers quickly answer and lose control of the sale. That's not good news.

Catch Me if You Can

Instead, you want to take control once you've broken the ice on the phone. Quickly and politely ask them what's happened so far. Just like you would if you watched the second episode of "Line of Duty" without watching the first one. You would either watch the summary piece at the beginning or ask your partner what happened.

It's the same concept. Find out:

1. Who else have they spoken to?

2. What sites have they visited?

3. What solutions have they already considered, and why have they discounted them?

4. What problems led them to look into a solution?

5. What brought them to your site or aggregator?

6. What do they already know about you or your firm? What did they like about you? Or not like?

7. How important is solving the problem to them? What's the impact of doing nothing?

8. How much are they considering spending on the solution?

9. What options are on the top of their list at the moment? What was the cost of these? How did they feel about that?

You'll not be able to ask all these questions, but if you take your time, build a rapport, settle them down, and explain why you want to know, you can get away with numerous questions. Explain why you're asking the questions and that you want to help them as much as possible, but you need to find out where they are so far before you can help.

Qualifying the Customer

We've already started this process with our "catching up" questions. Let's do this properly. Any enquiry or potential customer needs to be qualified. To a certain degree, the customer, having to leave their name, email address, and phone number on a website to receive a call, tells me they are pretty motivated to do something about solving their problem or achieving their goal.

So use MANT to ensure they are suitably qualified:

- M – Motivation – are they motivated to do something about their needs?

- A – Ability – Do they have the ability to do something. Can they afford it, obtain finance, clear a credit check, have a property with equity? These questions probably come later in your explore segment

- N – Need – Do they have a need? Our regulator wants us to establish a need and later put this in our suitability letter. All financial products must meet a recognised need; otherwise, you're mis-selling.

- T – Timescale – Are they wanting to do this now or later. What's driving them to do it now? What's the urgency?

Your Sales Process

Once you've caught up with them, introduce them to your sales process, advice process, or whatever you want to call it. Share with them the next steps and how you will help them. Remember they have called you for some extra help and agreed to a call, so gain permission to spend some quality time with them on the phone.

Signpost the following steps, which probably look like this: explore needs, research solution, present solution, complete application or next steps. Please don't get too complex with this or overthink it. Selling or advising is quite simple. You find out what they need, convert this to want by building desire, present your solution showing how it solves their problem, hits their goals, and then creates the urgency to get it moving quickly.

That's it – don't overthink it.

Pre-empting Concerns Particularly the Rate and Fee Question

The final technique to ensure you succeed from most of your calls is to consider the small problem of "client concerns" or customer objections as we used to call them. All customers will have reservations when they buy anything. Just because you advise (sell) regulated products such as mortgages, homeowner loans or bridging, doesn't mean people buy them without any questions or concerns. They will have these.

Furthermore, your product or service might spring additional concerns which the customer wasn't expecting. For example, you may sell homeowner loans secured as a second charge on the property. The problem you might face is the fees and interest rates charged. Compared to a low loan to value mortgage on a residential property, the rates and fees are higher because:

- The lender risk is more significant; they only have the second charge or priority on the property. Hence a higher rate to build a margin.

- Often the loan leaves very little equity in the property; some Second Charges can be lent up to 90% or more. House prices falling can leave the lender in a precarious position. Besides, high loan to value first mortgages without the government guarantee can be priced at 4% plus nowadays as the lender takes more risk.

- Remember, the customer will be comparing your solution to the mortgage they currently have or have had in the past, which may be on a low percentage.

- There are costs involved that you meet in your fee—valuation of the property, legal conveyancing fees and such. On a high-value property, these can be expensive—£1,000 for a valuation plus similar legal costs.

- Because the loan is secured against the property, the lender can lend "long" – 10 plus years, which will bring the monthly payment down dramatically, and it's this that really matters to the customer. Many have short redemption penalties to be redeemed and replaced by a first charge mortgage later.

- Second lenders often help borrowers that first charge lenders would not consult. Self-employed, those with unusual income, those with blemishes on their credit record. These customers pose a higher risk, so the lender needs to build a margin to offset the increased re-possession risk—hence higher interest rates.

- You have systems and infrastructure, allowing you to move the application on very quickly and get the money in their bank account within days rather than months. This is very useful.

- The lender can secure a bridging loan on a couple of properties rather than one, allowing your customer to enter your bid at auction or complete it quickly, thus saving money. The lender has the legal capability and infrastructure to do this in-house, saving time.

The list goes on, and I'm sure you can add much more.

Right now, you think that there are plenty of benefits here and that the lender is in their right mind to charge a higher rate of interest. You can set a fee to cover your costs and benefits without remorse.

The Secret Sauce

Let the customer know about these issues before telling them the rate and fee. You must disclose the fee, obviously – it would be immoral and illegal not to, but make sure you shower them with benefits as you do so. You ski downhill, not uphill. Help them appreciate that there will be fees and a higher interest rate before they know what this is.

And adding them to the loan can certainly ease cash flow.

Besides, a second charge homeowner loan can leave your first mortgage intact, thus removing the need to redeem it and incur an eye-watering redemption penalty, which many lenders still get away with.

Another helpful technique to handle the price/fee concern is to find out what the customer is comparing this to in their experience. Ask the question:

"What are you comparing these to?" Wait patiently, use softening techniques, and the customer will tell you what's in their head. Probably the cost of their original first mortgage, i.e. 4% and the fee of £250. Knowing this will allow you to justify your fee quickly.

But doing it before they object is best. Always.

The restaurant that charges top prices won't shock its customers. But they will pre-empt or allow the customer to know the bill will be high. The frontage will look expensive, the décor will shine, the maître d'. will be competent, the menu will display the prices in beautiful calligraphy, the social media presence will scream out expensive, and the food will be delightful. A Michelin Star will help too.

Beware

However, one thing to be careful of when dealing with concerns and pre-empting them is that you may fear suggesting them. Even if they hadn't thought of them first. Shelley recently had her COVID vaccine jab; she was very nervous about the side effects, who isn't, so when the nurse asked her if she was aware of the side effects, she said, "don't tell me as I know I'll have them all".

Line of Duty starts tonight; I'd better watch the first episode to know what's happening next. Remember this next time you make a call to a "bought" lead. It's all in the catching up.

Using Behavioural Styles to Influence Your Client

Chapter Summary

Paul outlines a blueprint to speed up your mortgage advising by drilling into different customers and how they operate. By understanding how people "tick" quickly and correctly, you can communicate and influence them in a just-right manner. This creates rapport, trust and a long-term relationship.

Before we start, I'd like you to complete the questionnaire below to assess your colour style. All will be revealed as you progress this chapter.

The Colours – Social Styles - A Personal Profile

How can you tell what your own behavioural style is? The following questionnaire will help you analyse your behaviour according to the four behavioural styles. As you'll learn once you have scored your responses, some will fall into other quadrants. Remember, this profile simply highlights your most frequent tendencies.

There are no right or wrong answers in this questionnaire. This survey enables you to describe the style you use in your relationships with others.

There are twenty statements on the following pages, each followed by four different endings. For each statement, indicate the ending that best describes your behaviour in a work environment. In some cases, two choices may seem equally like you; please choose the one most like your behaviour most of the time.

When you've completed the questionnaire, score your answers according to the directions on the subsequent page.

Questions

1.   I am likely to impress others as:

    a   practical and to the point

    b   emotional and somewhat stimulating

    c   supportive and dependable

    d   intellectually orientated and rather serious

2. In communicating with others, I may:

    a   tendency to ignore those who talk about "long-range" and direct my attention to what needs to be done right now.

    b   show impatience with ideas that show little originality.

    c   show little interest in those whose opinions are obviously not thought through and therefore risky.

    d   express frustration with those who do not have their facts straight.

3. Sometimes, I suspect I may come across to others as being:

    a   too dominating and too intensive

    b   too emotional or too overly dramatic

    c   too agreeable or too pliable

    d   overly concerned with specifics to the point of being nit-picking

4. When I am working on a project, I want to:

    a   work with people who want to get results quickly.

    b   work with people who are creative and interested in innovation.

    c   be stimulated and involved with people

    d   have time to gather facts and make sure the project develops systematically and logically.

5. In any organisation, I like to:

    a   be giving orders or working independently. I don't want to waste time on "how are we going to do this". I just want to do it.

    b   give my opinions. I can take advice from people already successful in the area, not those with no "track record".

    c   work collaboratively with people, not alone. I can accept advice and direction from approving authorities.

    d   make my own decisions based on the facts at hand. I can take direction if I understand the logic behind it.

6.   When circumstances prevent me from doing what I want, I tend to:

   a   review the situation for any deficiencies on my part and take action accordingly.

   b   create a new hypothesis quickly.

   c   analyse the motivation of others and develop a fresh feel for the situation.

   d   keep in mind all the basics or history to date and pinpoint all key obstacles. I modify my plan after much thinking.

7.   When I write an email for business to someone I don't know, I usually try to:

   a   relate my purpose in writing and highlight what I want, need or expect of them.

   b   show my main points and how they work toward the future goals we both have.

   c   convey some of who I am and my style.

   d   give the background and purpose of the communication in some detail.

8.   In terms of how I think about time, I usually concentrate on:

   a   my immediate actions and whether they work for today.

   b   my long-range goals and how to get there. I'm not very disciplined with time.

   c   how what I'm planning may affect other people.

   d   ensuring the actions I take fit into the systematic program I've set up.

9.   When I meet people behaviourally, I am likely to consider whether:

   a   they know what they're doing and can get things done.

   b   they're exciting and creative.

   c   friendly and open.

   d   they seem thoughtful and reflective.

10.   When faced with people who hold a different point of view, I usually try to:

   a   rely on my ability to pull ideas together and convince others of my ideas.

   b   find several places we agree on to build on these and move forwards.

   c   place me in their shoes and see their point of view.

   d   keep my composure and help others see things logically.

11. If I were to speak before a group that didn't know me well, I would hope to leave the impression of being.

   a   a pragmatic "mover" who could assist the group in solving problems.

   b   a broad-range thinker capable of making innovative contributions.

   c   a lively person clearly in touch with the group's mood and needs, thus able to help make an impact.

   d   a systematic thinker who could help the group analyse its problems and needs.

12. In tense meetings, I occasionally:

   a   attempt to bulldoze my opinion because I'm frustrated by the process.

   b   let my hair down and express feelings better left unsaid.

   c   am swayed by others who may be solid personalities but not necessarily correct in the situation.

   d   miss the forest for the trees because I get caught in the details.

13. Sometimes, when my behaviour seems extreme, others might feel I am:

   a   dominating, brutal or harsh.

   b   moody, excitable or unpredictable.

   c   dependent, conforming or unsure.

   d   highly unemotional or detached.

14. I feel satisfied with myself when I:

   a   get more things accomplished than I've planned.

   b   develop new thoughts and create ideas that can be implemented.

   c   understand and respond in a helpful way to the feelings of others.

   d   solve a problem using a logical method.

15. I find I am most convincing when I can:

   a   present options to people and help them choose an alternative.

   b   stimulate people with new ideas and excite them into action.

   c   be in touch with my own feelings and empathise with those of others

   d   use logic and facts to persuade people to my point of view.

16. When others pressure me, I am inclined to be overly:

   a   concerned with proving myself with immediate action.

   b   emotional and get carried away with my feelings.

   c   concerned with what others think and tend not to take action

   d   analytical and critical of others.

17. Under challenging situations, my approach sometimes results in being:

   a   too concerned with here and now and getting and doing what I want.

   b   so worried about settling the battle and getting to the future that I misjudge the present situation.

   c   so concerned about others that I don't think through my own situation.

   d   too involved with concepts and ideas alone.

18. I like it when others tell me they think I'm:

   a   a person who knows where they are going and is going to get there.

   b   creative and stimulating.

   c   a dependable person who comes through for them.

   d   Intellectually gifted.

19. When there's interference on a project, I usually think it's best to:

   a   concentrate on getting what I want to be accomplished right now.

   b   be original and say what I think.

   c   find out how others feel and make sure we agree on a procedure.

   d   stick to a logical, systematic, proven approach.

20. Overall, I would describe myself as:

   a   pragmatic and forceful.

   b   stimulating and creative.

   c   willing and supportive.

   d   thoughtful and industrious.

Scoring

Add up each A, B, C and D you've noted and place in the first column.

A.......... x 5 = ...%

B.......... x 5 = ...%

C.......... x 5 = ...%

D.......... x 5 = ...%

Total 20   Total 100%

Now, multiply each of your totals by 5 to determine the percentage you scored in each category and place these numbers in the second column.

For example:

A   5 x 5   = 25%

B   12 x 5   = 60%

C   3 x 5   = 15%

D   0 x 5   = 0%

Total 20   Total 100%

Interpretation

Each category, as you've probably suspected, correlates to one of the behavioural styles:

A = Red Drivers

B = Yellow Expressive

C = Blue Amiable

D = Green Analytical

In the example above, the person is primarily a yellow expressive (60%) with a strong red driver component (25%), some blue amiable (15%) and no green analytical.

Why We Need to Adapt to People?

When all is said and done, and believe me, more is said than done; people buy people. Clients need to trust you and work with you, especially in professional services such as mortgage and protection advising. Liking you would be a great goal, too, although not essential. However, it makes the job far more enjoyable when you like your client and she feels the same way; after all, life is too short.

Trust is key. Part of trust is being similar, speaking on the same wavelength, and having things in common. This is human nature and has been prevalent for thousands of years. Advisers need to feel this with their clients. The easiest and simplest way of achieving this is to become more adept at fathoming people out and adapting how you deal with people.

The Two Needs of Clients

We deal with mortgage and protection advising clients. Usually one or two people, so it's much easier to connect with them. Your client will have two needs:

1.   Product or advice needs

2.   Personal needs

Advice needs are out of this chapter's scope and are something that your training and education have prepared you for. Personal needs are a different need altogether.

People want to be handled in a certain way, communicated uniquely, perceived differently. Some want to connect warmly; some want to research more beforehand; others want you to get to the point.

Much of this we deal with instinctively; we change, chameleon ourselves to adapt to people as they present themselves. It bears no real thinking because we intuitively do it. But on occasions, we get it wrong, we handle someone as we've always done, but we don't seem to connect, we're not in tune with them, there's no chemistry.

Leaving it to chance or instinct is fine. Still, if you want to get it right every time or gauge people very early to sever the relationship quickly, you need a tool.

The Social Styles Colours

We have the Social Style Colours. Simple to use, fun to exhibit and more importantly, extremely powerful and successful.

Integral to our understanding and use is my ABC

1. A – assess their style;

2. B – borrow their style,

3. C – communicate in their style.

To assess their style, let's look at you first to help you understand how the model works.

Social Style Colours – Assessing Your Customer

Quickly

Take a piece of paper and draw a vertical line with arrows on either end.

Now put at the top "Task and goal-focused" and at the bottom "people-focused". Gauge someone you know from work or a customer or client along this line. How goal-focused are they compared with being more concerned around people? Put an "X" where they might appear.

Next, a horizontal line cutting through the middle. On the left side, mark it "Introvert or ask," and on the right side ", extrovert or tell." Again mark an "X" where you think your person appears along the line.

"Tell" people are easy to spot – they just go around talking much of the time with few questions in their language. "Ask" people are also easy to see – they don't speak as much, and when they do, they are more interested in seeking the views of others through asking questions.

Some people like to use introvert and extravert for the exact dimensions. I like this. I'm pretty introverted, preferring to listen to people rather than talkaholic. I ask more questions to encourage this. Equally, I know extroverts who keep talking and raising the energy of groups and meetings.

Task

Introvert ← → **Extrovert**

People

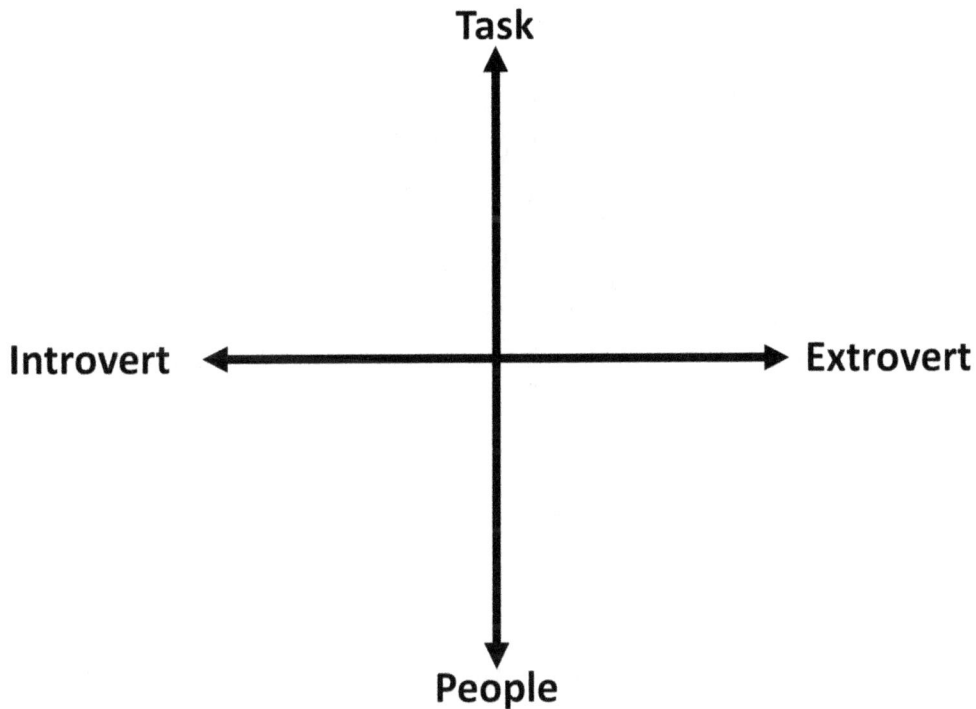

The Styles - Explained

We start to put people in these boxes from the behaviour we see from our observations.

We're not character analysing them, getting hyper psychological with this, or doing any kind of therapy; we're just figuring people and customers out a little.

I am trying to fathom what makes them tick and why. Simple, quick and easy to apply to anyone you meet.

To simplify our descriptions, I've given each box colour like this:

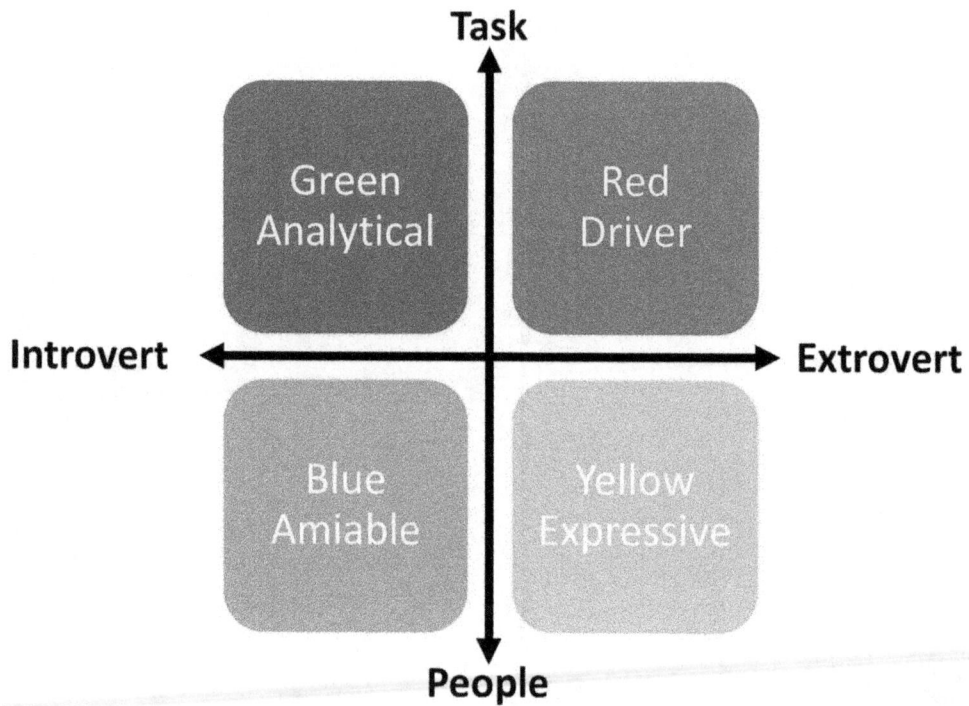

Let's describe the characteristics more and put down keywords for each colour.

Green Analytical

- Reflective
- Cautious
- Precise
- Formal
- Rules-led
- Detailed

Red Drivers

- Competitive
- Strong-willed
- Dynamic

- Decisive
- Action

Amiable Blue

- Intimate
- Caring
- Supportive
- Trusting
- Encouraging

Expressive Yellow

- Talkative
- Sociable
- Enthusiasts
- Group-oriented
- Influential
- Collaborative
- Flexible

Some Important Caveats

You can easily cross over lines and be half of one or another colour. I tend to cross over the bottom line and have some green in me plus blue, i.e., analytic and amiable, but I do have more green in me, though.

You can move quickly; we encourage that in our ABC – assess, borrow, communicate – so borrow someone else's colour and become a Smart Blue or a Smart Red. Borrowing is temporary; it's not personal and is designed to speed along the rapport and help you communicate with the customer. It smooths the wheels of communication; it is not false to who you are; this is simply a way to get on with people more, not a character analysis exercise.

I tend to use the Colours in a work setting, i.e., when I meet them in business. You can do this with a home setting if you want; it doesn't matter. You're assessing their behaviour as you see it. All it needs to be is true to them.

Oddly they might be borrowing another colour's style without even knowing they're doing so. Make sure you assess their normal behaviour. Also, care they are not in conflict with a situation or person. This changes people's behaviour to a more extreme version, so it is not helpful to use.

Influencing Each Colour

We've done the A; now we're doing the B and C – the borrowing and communicating in their style. What are the dos and don'ts?

Look at this comprehensive list and see if you recognise any traits of people you know.

Influencing Green Analytical

- Provide facts and data in a logical, organised format.

- Don't be disorganised or messy.

- Approach them in a straightforward, direct way.

- Stick to business.

- Don't joke, be casual, informal or loud.

- Support their principles.

- Use a thoughtful approach to build your credibility by listing the pros and cons of any suggestions you make.

- Don't rush the decision-making process.

- Contribute to their efforts.

- Present specifics, and do what you say you can do.

- Don't be vague about what is expected of either of you.

- Do not fail to follow through.

- Take your time, but be persistent.

- Don't waste time.

- Draw up a scheduled approach to delivery; assure them there will be no surprises.

- Don't leave things to chance or luck. If you agree, follow through.

- Don't threaten, persuade or coax.

- If you disagree, make an organised presentation of your position.

- Don't use testimonies of others or unreliable sources. Give them time to verify the reliability of your actions.

- Be accurate and realistic.

- Don't use other people's opinions as evidence.

- Provide solid, tangible, practical evidence.

- Don't use gimmicks or clever manipulators.

- Give them time to be thorough.

- Don't push too hard or be unrealistic with deadlines.

Influencing Red Drivers

- Be clear, specific, brief and to the point.

- Don't ramble on or waste their time.

- Stick to business.

- Don't try to build a personal relationship.

- Come prepared with all their requirements in a well organised "package".

- Don't be disorganised or messy.

- Do not confuse or distract their mind from the business.

- Present the facts logically and concisely.

- Don't leave loopholes or vague issues.

- Ask specific (preferably "what") questions

- Don't ask rhetorical or irrelevant questions.

- Provide alternatives and choices for them to make their own decisions.

- Don't come with a ready-made decision, and do not decide for them.

- Provide facts and figures about the probability of success of effectiveness of options

- Don't speculate wildly or offer guarantees and assurances if you can't be sure.

- If you disagree, take issues with facts, not the person.

- If you disagree, do not let it reflect on them personally.

- If you agree, support the results, not the person.

- Motivate and persuade by referring to objectives and results.

- Don't try to convince by "personal means."

- Support their conclusions.

- Don't direct or order

- After finishing business, leave quickly.

- Don't stay for a personal chat after business.

Influencing Blue Amiables

- Start with a personal comment; break the ice.

- Don't rush into business or the schedule.

- Show interest in them as people, find areas of common interest, and be candid and open.

- On the other hand, don't stick solely to business; on the other hand, do not lose sight of goals by being too personal.

- Draw out personal objectives and work to help achieve these.

- Listen and be responsive.

- Don't force them to respond to your objectives; do not say, "This is how I see the situation."

- Present your case softly, in a non-threatening manner.

- Don't be overbearing or demanding; do not threaten them with position power.

- Ask "how" questions to draw out their opinions.

- Don't debate about facts and figures.

- Observe for possible areas of early disagreement or dissatisfaction.

- Don't manipulate or bully them into agreeing because they probably will not fight back.

- If you disagree, look for hurt feelings and changes in attitude.

- Behave casually and informally.

- Don't be abrupt and rapid.

- Define clearly, preferably in writing, individual contributions.

- Don't be vague.

- Do not offer options and probabilities.

- Reassure that their decision will minimise risks and emphasise the benefits.

- Don't offer assurances and guarantees you cannot fulfil.

- Provide personal assurances.

- Give clear, specific solutions with maximum guarantees.

Influencing Yellow Expressives

- Support their dreams and intuitions.

- Don't lay down the law or suppress their opinions.

- Don't be dogmatic.

- Leave time for socialising.

- Don't be curt, cold or tight-lipped.

- Talk about people and their objectives; they find opinions stimulating.

- Don't concentrate on facts and figures, alternatives, abstractions, or detail.

- Get their commitment to a course of action.

- Don't leave decisions up in the air.

- Ask for their opinions and ideas about people.

- Don't waste time trying to be impersonal, business-like, task-orientated.

- Provide ideas for carrying out decisions.

- Control "dreaming" with them, or you will lose time.

- Use enough time to be stimulating, fun-loving, fast-moving.

- Don't mess around too much; don't stick too rigidly to the plan either.

- Don't talk down to them; do not patronise.

Social Style Needs Summary

	Green Analytical	Blue Amiable	Red Driver	Yellow Expressive
Primary Asset	Systematic	Supportive	Focused	Energising
Back-up Behaviour	Avoid	Acquiesce	Autocratic	Attack
For Growth Needs to	Decide	Initiate	Listen	Check
Strongest Personal Motivator	Respect	Approval	Results	Recognition
Needs Climate That	Describes	Supports	Commits	Collaborates
Let Them Save	Face	Relationships	Time	Effort
Try to be	Accurate	Agreeable	Efficient	Stimulating
Support Their	Principles and thinking	Relationships and feelings	Conclusions and actions	Visions and intuitions
For Decisions Give Them	Data and evidence	Assurances and guarantees	Options and probabilities	Testimony and incentives
Follow up with	Service	Support	Action	Attention

Mortgage Advising with Analytical Amin (Green)

Analytical Amin asks many questions and seems interested in a lot of detail. He has already researched the various options and wants to learn about mortgages and protection. He queried the Initial Disclosure and was particularly interested in your authorisation as an Appointed Representative.

What extra steps would you now take to handle Amin?

- Allocate more time to my meetings.

- Perhaps split the further meetings into smaller chunks online.

- Share the background more and the rationale behind your recommendations.

- Use more logic in your descriptions and analysis.

- Be slightly more formal in your approach, less humour and jokes.

- Pull back on the small talk and need to build a rapport; Amin wants to trust you, not like you.

- Use more test closes to assess how Amin is, whether he's understanding.

- Give him time to make decisions in the mortgage recommendation.

- Send some research in advance for him to study, maybe some web links so he can see where you're researching. Specifically, their website and other links prove why the lender is chosen.

- Show him how you've arrived at the protection "gap" on the protection side. Show him the calculations and data that helped you conclude that he needs protection.

- Ask him for the implications of maintaining the gap but using logical next step, outcome, reaction, significance rather than "feeling" words.

- Above all, don't rush him or put him in a corner to make decisions.

- Layout, the following steps and sequence of events, Amin will love that.

Mortgage Advising with Expressive Eloise (Yellow)

It isn't easy to get back on track as she is pretty happy to wander off in her conversation. It's 30 minutes into the meeting, and we haven't even started the factfind. What should I do differently now:

- Politely bring things back on track and keep her aware of the timing.

- Allow time to digress and build a rapport with her.

- When discussing protection, use a lifeline exercise to discover her past, present and future around property, family and work.

- Find ways to naturally compliment her, as expressive yellows love to feel good and are admired and respected by other people, even their financial advisers. Don't worry about being sycophantic in your eyes; she will see it as genuine.

- Bring in her examples of family and people she knows who will be impacted by her illness or death.

- Take more control, signpost and guide her along the process.

- Utilise some client testimonials to elicit her commitment to proceed. Peer pressure and case studies will move her. Personal opinions of your work.

- Drive the agenda but don't stick too rigidly to it.

- Above all, please help her decide; a soft close would work well.

Mortgage Advising with Amiable Alain (Blue)

You've moved very swiftly through the factfind meeting, finding yourself further ahead than usual. Have you missed anything? No, but Alain does appear quiet. They're full of smiles but just are not saying much. What should you do?

- Start bringing them into the conversation more, drawing their opinions or views as you progress. Ask more open questions and remember to "sugar coat" your questions with a good tone and pre-frames.

- Dampen down the formality; try and turn more casual in your approach.

- Watch their body language, read their facial expressions to gauge their interest or understanding.

- Spend some time building a rapport with Alain. Try and find things in common.

- Match and mirror them as far as you can. Posture, energy levels, eye contact, expressions.

- Please slow down and deviate a little to bring in their opinions.

- De-risk your solutions.

Mortgage Advising with Dani Driver (Red)

She does come across as rather austere and decisive. She knows what she wants that's obvious, and you can't relax the situation or feel too much at ease. You don't think there's a rapport. How should you continue?

- By recognising that she is not like you and accepting that you will not necessarily be friends.

- Start to drive a strict schedule, keep timings, and get moving along your sales process.

- Don't deviate, use too many personal stories and examples; stick to the facts

- Act confident and assured. Professional and efficient.

- Ask about their goals and objectives unless you already have them. Chunk up the goals away from small objectives. Talk big picture.

- Complement Dani genuinely with a link to her objectives and goals.

- Try not to wallow in too much detail unless you have to. If something is detailed, always refer to the bigger goal this area contributes to.

- Dry up the personal chat and need to be liked. Finish the meeting in time, preferably before time, never over-run.

- Please get to the point quicker with your descriptions. Read body language to assess patience levels or lose interest. Speed things up.

- Help them decide by asking them to go ahead; you'll be surprised about their decisiveness if the solution meets their goals.

Building Trust with Clients

Why Trust is Super Important Right Now

Last night I was having a healthy supper and an equally healthy debate about the trials and tribulations of working from home. We both agreed that being based at home was no longer an issue, and if your work involves a laptop, your brain and cloud data, then you can work anywhere.

The honest debate started over Zoom Video calls or phone calls to prospects and customers. Shelley's response and she happens to be a fan of the phone, was, "they don't need to see me; I have a big brand behind me."

And it's true. Her company dominates the space she's involved in and has a tremendous local reputation that has taken years to ferment.

The same is true for Nationwide Building Society, Prudential and Virgin Money, which is why these firms will do well in the artificial intelligence selling market, Robo advising and Arti type chatbots. Nationwide dealt with a massive proportion of its chat enquiries over payment holidays using its automated chat service.

You may not be so lucky to have such a brand behind you. You may not be known in your marketplace, so you need to work hard and spend time building trust and your reputation.

Here's a reminder on how to do that:

- Sprinkle your credibility all over social media and the internet. Make sure your LinkedIn profile is complete, blogs are populated with your writings, and your YouTube Channel has some excellent videos about you and your service.

- Have a Zoom background with your certificates and exam rewards.

- Ensure your testimonials are gathered somewhere for people to see. Your website or, better still, a third-party site such as vouchedfor, or unbiased.co.uk or www.financiable.co.uk

- Nail the three secrets to trust – common ground, credibility and intent.

- Matching is a great place to start. I have videos on this topic on my YouTube Channel www.paularcher.tv – or just become a little bit like your customer. That means facial expressions, eye contact, voice matching, pace and energy on a video.

- Outlining your intentions is often forgotten. Ensure your customer knows what you're about, why do you do what you do. How your sales process works, how long you'll speak for and so on. Signpost your video calls, so customers know where you're going.

- Learn to be a masterful communicator online.

High trust is paramount but can be broken in an instance.

CIC Them First

"You've got to CIC them before you do anything else" were the immortal words uttered from my very first sales manager at the Prudential Insurance Company of Great Britain. He was one of the most exemplary life assurance salespeople you could've met. Very old school now, naturally since this was mid-1980's, all gloss and shiny shoes, but he could sell insurance.

"You can't kick your customers?" I responded.

"I don't mean kick Paul; I mean CIC. CIC are the 3 secrets to reducing tension and building trust with your customers, and you have to make sure you've CIC'ed them before you meet and in the first ten minutes or so of meeting them. That way, you can reduce the natural tension they have with you and build the trust which helps you to connect."

We've all heard of the need to build trust rapport and become liked. Maybe the last one is a bit old school sales. Still, the pure fact is your customer is not going to open up to you, answer the provocative questions you're going to ask and reveal their world to you unless you have the 3 elements of trust nailed.

Let me explain each one and make some suggestions on building this. But before we start, can I ask you to jot down or say in your head the typical questions your customer might have about you and the meeting that you've arranged as they park their car and walk towards your office. Think about how they've found you as well.

Did you cold call them, were they referred from an existing client or referred by someone in your company?

Questions customers think about. Here's some I prepared earlier:

- I wonder what they'll be like?
- I hope they don't force me to buy something.
- Will I like them?
- What will this all cost?
- I hope I can afford it?
- Will they listen to me?

- Will they know what they're talking about?

- How long will this take?

Let's put those questions aside and explain CIC. C stands for commonality, which of course, we've all heard of before. Having something in common with someone is the secret to becoming liked. Do we need to be appreciated and liked? Probably not, but I think it makes the engagement a lot more enjoyable.

My daughter calls them BFFs. This stands for best friend forever. Think about your best friend; what do you like about them, why are they your best friend. Mine has a lot in common with me. It's all quite natural. So how can we establish some commonality in the first ten minutes?

CIC – Common Ground

Don't Forget Common Ground

One of the advantages of your favourite Premier League Football team playing erratically is that you can buy tickets for home matches. And so this happened for me at Manchester United's Old Trafford ground.

With my two teenage sons, we ventured to Manchester with our tickets for the first time. Unfortunately, we were unable to secure three consecutive seats. My two boys sat next to each other, but I was a couple of seats behind them on my own.

However, we were amongst fellow fans, and I soon became ensconced in conversation about Manchester United past and present with my two adjoining new friends. We spoke about Eric Cantona's brilliance, Sparky's incisiveness in attack and Steve Bruce's staunch defensiveness. Plus, Schmeichel's antics in front of the goal.

We were all soon best buddies.

Doesn't it just prove the value of common ground? I know it's a cliché, but do you still seek common ground with your customers and clients. It's one of the rapport-building techniques that will live forever.

Didn't Oasis want to "Live Forever"?

Enough of the Manchester connections, my friends in Liverpool will never let me live that down. Oh, I forgot, we won the match 1:0, very rare for Manchester United at the moment.

Match their Voice to Maximise Rapport

One of my favourite accents comes from Southern Louisiana, USA. Slow, drawling, and rhythmic. Try to copy it, and it sounds terrible. Like the Ant Hill Mob driver in the Whacky Races or Tinker in Speed Buggy. YouTube both of those that if you don't remember.

This person, probably from New Orleans, has grown up with others from the same area who sound the same or comparable. Their parents appeared similar and probably gave them their accent in the first place. So, for them to hear an identical voice must be nectar for their ears.

We can't and mustn't imitate an accent – that's mimicry.

But we can match the voice. Three areas to match.

1. Volume or loudness.

2. Pace or speed.

3. Resonance or deepness.

The trick is to listen carefully, fathom out where their voice comes from. Does it emanate from the throat? Kind of nasally.

Or from the top of the stomach.

Or from deep below, under the stomach. Resonant and deep like a trombone.

Now make your voice come from the same place, and you'll be amazed how accurately you'll begin to match their sound without mimicking them at all.

High up in the throat – fast and high pitched. Low down deep in the abdomen is low timbre and slow. The middle of the stomach is medium paced and toned. Try it; it works.

Do this, and the person you're talking to will feel right at home rather than talking to a stranger.

Or was it Penelope Pitstop from Wacky Races? Now there's a blast from the past, and Peter Perfect was always on hand to rescue that lil ol' lady.

The Power of Rapport

It could've ended in a disaster and an international debacle except for a little thing called rapport.

10 US Navy sailors were detained after one of their two vessels broke down during a training mission in the Gulf in late 2015. Those incarcerated - nine men and one woman - were taken to Farsi Island, where Iran has a naval base in the middle of the Gulf.

US Secretary of State John Kerry called Foreign Minister Javad Zarif shortly after the incident. The pair developed a personal rapport during the nuclear talks.

As a result, Iranian state media said the group was released into international waters after apologising. The incursion was "unintentional", a statement from the Revolutionary Guards quoted by state media.

Now that's the power of rapport. Here are some tips to remind you how.

- Seek common ground

- Maintain eye contact and a respectful distance

- Smile copiously

- Compliment the other person genuinely

- Match their thinking styles – visual, auditory, kino

- Match energy levels

- Match physiology

CIC – Intent

"I" stands for intent or your intention. Humans, unsurprisingly, trust only one person. And that person is themselves; we mistrust others and are wary of their true intention. Your customer will wonder what your real intention is and might expect the worse; after all, you're a salesperson.

Yet many of us expect the customer to assume our intention is right and honourable. Since your intention is always honest, we should let them know this. Do you have a higher purpose? All of us should in our professional lives.

Of course, we want to make a profit for our businesses and feed our families, but what's your higher purpose beyond all of that? Mine became apparent when I dealt with my first death claim as a life assurance salesman. After that moment, I knew that my higher purpose was to provide protection for families. In the event of the worse happening to them, they would have the cushion and comfort of money coming into the household to somehow rebuild their lives. Taking the lack of money off the table, they could re-build.

This drove my real purpose and intention, and I let my customers know this right at the front of our meeting.

CIC – Competency

The final C stands for competency. How competent or good are you at what you do. We are fully qualified with all the examinations and continued professional development we have to do nowadays. This is not just technical ability but your skill in communicating, guiding, suggesting, listening. Experience, wisdom.

How to Show Your Competence

One of the advisers I most admired in my career was a broker called Joss. Behind her desk, in eye view of her clients, was a collage of thank you cards from all her satisfied clients. All her new clients would see these, read a few and immediately feel comfortable with Joss and her competence.

My desk was immediately beneath an enormous sign saying "Prudential Property Services" in my first sales role. I relied on the brand to set a solid first impression.

Gone are the days when new customers could rely on the brand to demonstrate how competent you are. Halifax, Lloyds, Santander names all give an impression that usually shows that any adviser working for them knows a thing or two about mortgages.

Their advice days are withering, and you may be encountering lots of new customers as an independent mortgage adviser. One of the fundamental challenges will be proving your competence in the first 10 minutes without relying on a significant brand name above your head.

Here are eight ideas to help you do this before you meet the client and within the first 10 minutes:

- Provide evidence for any definitive statements you use. If you're the number one broker in town, back it up somehow. If you're a whole market adviser, established for over ten years, show the client the FCA register entry or your Client Agreement brochure. Online via video, you can easily offer a screen share of the FCA register.

- If you've been associated in the finance industry or similar for many years, make sure you let your client know this to reflect your competence. Don't waffle on about it, but make sure they're aware of your years of experience.

- Exam certificates are helpful either as photos on the wall, as a visual on Zoom, maybe a background to use for a couple of minutes. Or just a PowerPoint slide showing your qualifications on video.

- Testimonials, endorsements and client reviews are more than helpful these days; they are essential. Your potential clients will look you up online and search for reviews of you and your firm. So long as they are impartial and logged in a reputable source, clients will feel assured of your capability and competence. Vouchedfor, unbiased, Google, Trustpilot – there are dozens to use.

- Testimonials and case studies on websites also work, especially if direct quotes from clients on the web pages. Video testimonials are most powerful and possibly a YouTube Channel with all sorts of videos demonstrating your competence.

- LinkedIn Profile is a must-have these days. You can own your name when it's searched on Google, which it will be. Purchase your name as a domain, for example, www.jenniferbarkley.me and have this redirected to your LinkedIn profile. Naturally, ensure your Social Selling Index is a high percentage with your profile.

- Podcasts demonstrate your expertise; a published book will do wonders to your silhouette. Articles in the trade press can help so long as you re-purpose these for your clients. Sponsorship may help; charity partnerships are also heart-warming.

- Finally, how you carry yourself off, communicate, explain things. How you use the tech if you're advising via video. What you look like also impacts, although this is not so important in these contemporary times. A suit and tie are a bit old fashioned, but that's a personal choice.

Awards? The British Mortgage Broker Award, the Intelligent Finance Magazine Award, the UK Financial Adviser Awards. Please don't get me on that bandwagon. Just think of the Eurovision song contest and the ultimate winners. Doesn't Lithuania constantly vote for Estonia, which also reciprocates and gives top marks to Latvia, who always supports Poland with the best marks? The UK always comes last, but surely we're the best. These are ego stroking lender marketing events all over LinkedIn like a rash and a complete waste of industry resources and money. If the funds were used to provide free training to every broker, that would be far more beneficial. The Award Ceremonies cost thousands of pounds.

Rant over.

Returning To Your Customer's Questions

Bring back those questions from earlier. Run through them and see which CIC is being sought. Let's have a look:

- I wonder what they'll be like? Commonality

- I hope they don't force me to buy something. Intent

- Will I like them? Commonality

- What will this all cost? Intent

- I hope I can afford it? Intent

- Will they listen to me? Competence

- Will they know what they're talking about? Competence

- How long will this take? Intent

I'll put some money on each of the questions you wrote down has one or more CIC attached.

Simple concepts, but essential to bringing success.

How To Read Body Language on Video

Chapter Summary

Paul takes an in-depth look at how you can read your customers' body language and facial expressions when online on video. When you realise how important this is for communication and buying signals, you'll see your customer very differently on video.

Paul shows you how to calibrate them, watch for small facial expression changes and hand to face.

With this peripheral visioning, you can move the advice forward and build a solid rapport even though you and the customer are virtual on video. Yes, it can be done.

Why Video?

You've taken the decision to promote online video communications with your customers and clients alike. Of course, you also offer face to face meetings, even a hybrid approach. Appeasing customer choices and preferences is key to a long-term relationship and having the option is good business practice.

As far as you're concerned, the professional adviser, working with customers mostly on video, makes sound sense. A boom for time management, easier to dissect the traditional hour-long meeting into smaller bite-sized sessions.

Simple to share documents, provide records of the meetings, and handle more clients than before. It saves time and money, is better for the environment and enables you to reach customers from far-flung places. Video is also better than phone since you can see each other clearly and use non-verbal signals to ferment the relationship.

But then traditions run deep.

- We've always done face to face.

- We have an expensive office suite and meeting rooms.

- Customers prefer face to face.

- It builds a better relationship.

I've heard all these arguments, and they are compelling.

An RDR Change Parallel

Sometimes it's in our bias, in our minds. We don't like change, prefer not to juggle tech, which always goes wrong anyway. I'm an adviser, not an IT wizard, you say. But all roles and professions change, and tech and the internet have encroached on just about every trade known. It's only really hitting us now. We need to embrace it. Here's a parallel to help you think this one through.

How long have you been in the sector? If you're an old hand, then you will remember commission. It dominated every aspect of financial service life, and the regulator didn't like it. They felt it encouraged mis-selling or at least product bias. They had a point.

When you advise on investments, a few unscrupulous advisers will favour the product that used to pay the highest commission.

Professionals kicked back voluntarily and pivoted over to a hybrid model of commission or fees. They gave the client a choice; let them decide. This is important – the customer could decide. The majority opted for the commission because that's what they were used to.

It worked ok, and the adviser beamed a smile of relief. Many advisers reluctantly switched to this hybrid model.

Then along came RDR, and by 1st January 2013, all investment advisers had to stop taking a commission and charge a fee. No longer was there a choice; it was all fees. Some advisers expected turmoil, disagreements, and locust infestation.

It didn't happen, advisers explained, clients agreed. Advice continued.

Back to Video

You see, when faced with one option, most of us can carry it through. If you give your client a choice of communication method, most customers will opt for the status quo face to face. Because that's the way, it's always been done.

If you only give the client one route and explain the benefits clearly, they'll opt for that. That's how you promote virtual on video advising.

The same happened when the broadcasting people shut off the analogue TV signal. Before people were given a choice, many still preferred their old BBC and ITV using the ariel that had stood on their roof for years. They didn't want to change. When they had to or were given little choice, they soon moved over and embraced the new and pin-sharp moving images.

Coaching your Customer

The first task is to make sure your video and tech work just fine. That's for another chapter. But for today, I want you to think about your customer's setup. If they're going to appear on video, you need to see them and hear them clearly.

They may need some coaching on this. They may not. Lockdown has self-taught millions of people to appear on Zoom, Facebook live, WhatsApp video and so on. Remember, these are consumers, not businesspeople mostly, so they may be unable to use Teams or Webex, designed for business types.

So you may need to have a few options up your sleeve.

Coach them before you start. Move their laptop closer, find a spot where there is light in front of them, not behind. Choose somewhere quiet. Check their microphone setup and their webcam image. Is it clear? A mortgage broker friend sends their client a complimentary headset to just plug into their laptop. This instantly produces excellent sound, and the client can hear clearly, too.

Cost around £30, so a valuable investment and cheaper than filling up the car with fuel to see the client.

Test Closing and Buying Signals

Now we can focus our attention on the significant benefits of having a video between you and your customer. You can read them, watch them. You've probably gotten quite used to reading body language over the years, picking up subtle signals to help you communicate.

We used to call these buying signals, which serves us well today.

If your client is happy with how things are progressing, then they'll accept your advice, and you can move forward to great results. As compliance people like to call it "a good or fair customer outcome".

An illustrative set of traffic lights helps enormously here. Have a set above your customer's head. When the session is going well, you're both in agreement, and there's lots of value – the lights are green.

When there's a misunderstanding or disjoint – the lights are amber. Red, naturally, is a big problem, but hopefully, you'll gauge this before it comes on.

Use test closes such as "how does this sound so far?" or "how is our meeting going for you?" and you'll soon see the traffic light change.

I'd now like to delve deeper into how you can read people online on video. It is very different to being with someone face to face, unsurprisingly. It's a learnt skill on video, but if their image and sound are good and yours are too, you can very quickly pick this up.

Calibrating Customers – There's a Tell for Everything

Before Lockdown, I was invited to deliver sales training for some clients in Dubai. It was over three days, and I trained over 60 people. Nothing unusual about that, but carting 60 sets of workbooks through the skies meant I had to take 2 large suitcases with me, one completely filled with workbooks.

Naturally, I still had two large suitcases on my return journey, again nothing odd there. But if you factor in that I was a businessman in a suit returning from a business trip in Dubai with two huge suitcases, it does start to look a little out of the ordinary.

The customs official at Heathrow airport thought so too and beckoned me over as I passed through customs. Here comes the suitcase search, I thought, thinking about missing my train home.

He began by asking me some odd questions:

"How are you today, Sir?" – Fine.

"Do these suitcases belong to you?" – Yes (obviously, since I was carrying them).

"Have you been to Dubai on business?" – Yes (obviously really since I was in a suit).

"Was it warm out there?" – Yes (obviously again, it's always warm in Dubai).

I soon figured out what he was doing. He observed me closely; looking at my physiology – body language, facial expressions – he studied my signals when I said "yes". I knew what he was going to do next. He would do the same thing with the word "no".

"Did you manage to get any sleep?" – No (obviously – it was a daytime flight of only 6 hours).

"Have you been doing any dangerous sports in Dubai, sir?" – No (good odds that most business meetings in Dubai don't involve bungee jumping)?

"Do you have anything in those cases that shouldn't be in there?" – No (this was the truth).

"Off you go then, Sir, and sorry to trouble you". And I left.

You see, he had calibrated my physiology for when I said no and was telling the truth. The body doesn't lie; there's a tell for everything, and he found it for the word "no", so he didn't even bother to search the case. Clever man.

The police do this, so do barristers in court. I do it with my three children, and I know when they're lying.

Remember physiology; there's always a tell for everything you do.

Thankfully I managed to catch my train home, it was a long, arduous journey, and I was keen to get the train, so thank you, NLP calibration, for helping me do this.

Peripheral Vision Focus

To read and look for subtle changes in facial expressions and body language, you've got to keep your eyes open. Whilst multitasking and making eye contact with your customer. This is obvious.

The problem with many advisers and people is that they stare at the camera. We're so scared of not looking at the lens if our customer doesn't believe we're engaged. This is dangerous so let me re-introduce you to the concept of peripheral vision.

My mum, God bless her soul, had a third eye. In the back of her head so she could see what my brothers and I were up to, whilst multitasking with the washing up and cooking. This is a metaphor because she didn't have a third eye, like Cyclops.

Foveal versus peripheral vision. If you're used to foveal, that's staring, then train yourself to go peripheral. Try this quick exercise.

Imagine a large dot in front of you may be on the far wall. Focus on that dot. Now, try to focus on everything around you without moving your stare. Keep your head still and don't move your eyes but continue to stretch your peripheral vision until you can naturally see 180 degrees from the spot.

Armed with peripheral vision capability, you can now look for leakage.

Recognising Leakage – Facial Expressions

He's retired now, but one of the most successful tennis champions of all time was a German fella named Boris Becker. He had a wicked serve that destroyed many an opponent, and for several years he was unassailable.

Until his arch-rival, Andre Agassi noticed something extraordinary.

He witnessed Boris leaking his body language. In fact, it was his facial expressions. He noticed that Boris would stick his tongue out very subtly to indicate which angle he would serve at. This gave Andre a split-second opportunity to move his position and return the sinful serve that was about to shoot across the net.

And it worked too.

Andre began to turn the tide of defeats and soon won all his matches against Boris. He was clever, though, not to let on, as he wanted to keep the secret to himself. He successfully evaded capture until they had both retired.

Have a look on YouTube; there's an insightful video with Andre explaining how he did it. Fascinating.

https://www.youtube.com/watch?v=57BMzCM6hQI

Recognising Hand to Face Gestures

Once we've calibrated our customer's everyday outlook, we can spot leakage. The easiest way to do this is via hand to face gestures.

You see, when on video, people still use their hands and arms for gesturing and the like. Not as commonplace as there is a perceived small gap between you and them, so people are sometimes reticent to use their hands.

But if their laptop or tablet is on a desk or table – which you should encourage rather than their lap – they will lean on the desk and will be free to use their hands.

Many of these gestures are intuitive. Here's a table of the most common.

Bored   Happy   Thinking

Thinking   Unsure   Thinking

Thinking   Thinking   Thinking

Body Language Quiz

Now time for a quiz. Look at the picture, cover the description and decide what's happening in the customer's mind. Then reveal the answer.

Trust your gut. Learn to honour your instincts in this; you are typically unconsciously correct. See how you get on.

Confident

Superiority

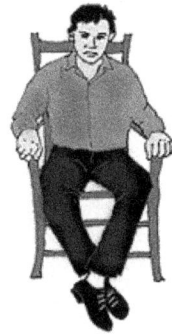

Dissatisfied or uncomfortable

Holding back strong feelings and emotions

Unhappy, angry and defensive

Contended, confident and smug

Self-satisfied and pompous person

Critical evaluation

"The Thinker"

"Let me consider"

Difficulty in concluding

"What was that again?"

Needs time to conclude

"Well, I don't know."

"I can't see it."

Steepling – confident and
knowledgeable

Sit-down readiness

Deep in troubled thought

Hot under the collar

Worried

Nervous

People who want to
consciously hide their
conversation

Rubbing wet palms against a
fabric communicates
nervousness

Hand to chest - conveys
loyalty, honesty and devotion

Using the Universal Emotions for Buying Signals

We're now in the business of reading our customer's facial expressions to gauge engagement and commitment. Intelligence Agencies around the world have been doing this for years.

Surveillance cameras can recognise people from a database of photos and read their expressions – sad, angry, intimidating.

This information is equally crucial to MI5 trying to rid the town of terrorists and police enforcers preventing crime.

How does a computer do this? Quite simply by memorising the Universal Emotions that humans all give to indicate their feelings. There are known facial expressions for each of the emotions:

- Sadness
- Anger
- Surprise
- Fear
- Disgust
- Contempt
- Happy

The Seven Dwarfs were probably based on these, but that was filmed in the 1940s. More recently, Eckman et al. has discovered the facial expressions that indicate them.

You can too. Here's how:

How to Read Emotions

1.   Log onto this website
     https://greatergood.berkeley.edu/quizzes/ei_quiz/take_quiz

2.   Do the quiz but remember to mirror the expression on the photo, and you will feel the emotion. Trust your gut.

Curing Yourself of the Three Listening Diseases

I mentioned earlier that the challenge is to read the body and facial language whilst looking out for leakage while conducting a regulated mortgage or financial services discussion. It's not easy to do it all at once.

This is why salespeople and advisers have listening diseases. See if you have any.

Listening Diseases and the Cure

1. Interruptitis
2. Interrogationitis
3. Premature Solutioneering

Have you ever been infected? All of us have been from time to time, we take a cure, but the disease is virulent and will return. Follow these tips to ensure you incubate yourself from all three in the future.

Interruptitis

My daughter, now 20, was inflicted with this in her early years. Kept interrupting her mother at the dinner table until she was told to stop disrupting. Meanwhile, her brain was not listening but storing up her next question or statement when her mother stopped talking.

I've seen salespeople influenced by this one since they've heard the same story over and over again, know all the answers, so just interrupt the customer before they've stopped talking. Take a mental pause and wait – ask yourself – why am I talking? Wait.

Interrogationitis

Many years ago, I had a first date and my keenness to get on and impress my new girlfriend led me to interrogate. So keen was I that I asked her lots of questions. One after the other. Accused of interrogation, we never progressed to a second date. Since then, I have learnt how to stop interrogating with questions.

Sugarcoating questions and chipping in with murmurings and snippets of words just to keep them talking. Verbal and non-verbal "nods" can keep the conversation going rather than endless questioning.

Premature Solutioneering

Closely affiliated to interruptitis with similar symptoms, except this one lets you finish their sentence. You're inclined to come in with your pre-prepared solution because you've heard the answer before. Let the client fully finish and explore further before you solve. Hold back your solution until you know for sure what the answer is.

Three diseases. You may recall having caught one or two. Remember to take medicine that Doctor Paul has prescribed; you'll be fine in the morning.

And the medicine is MAP, and here it is.

MAP'ing Your Success

During your virtual video meetings with customers, you'll want to really focus on them. Pick up body language, expressions, look for leakage and any emotions emanating.

So you can concentrate on this, I recommend you go into MAP mode when the customer is doing most of the talking. Which, by the way, should be most of the time if you're acting as a coach, not an adviser. Modern experts act as coaches, and I'll explain that another day.

What normally happens? You're kind of listening, but you quickly catch one of the diseases from earlier. Yuk. Instead MAP

M – Move Away From Doing Any Thinking

That's right, just stop thinking about what they tell you.

Of course, hear them and take it all in, but stop thinking about it. Prevent yourself thinking about your next question, calm yourself from figuring out the solution, halt yourself from interrupting them.

Let them talk. Remember though, you must:

A – Appreciate Them

Make it obvious you're listening intently, and you're interested. Show this in your body language, in your verbal assertions. "I see". "Really". "Do continue."

When they grind to a halt, and they will at some point. Simply:

P – Playback

What you heard them say, suggesting anything else you sensed or observed. Now you're tuned to pick up body language and senses, you'll be amazed at what you recognise.

Then they'll either speak some more or stop. Now you can ask another question. I occasionally run my MAP sessions for 10 to 15 minutes to elicit my customer's needs. Not only do I pick these up, but I get a great sense of their feelings, emotions and motivation.

Ideal in any sales related role.

Summary

Welcome to the virtual world of advising. It can be as good as face to face, never the same, of course, but equally beneficial to both parties.

Wait until virtual reality comes around. Pop your Ray-Bans on, the ones that Facebook, sorry Meta, have just sold you, and enter a virtual room where you can see all of your customers as if you were in the same room.

The metaverse is not far away, and learning to read body language virtually now will prepare you for any changes.

Your Mortgage Sales Process

Chapter Summary

Paul examines the need for a structured sales process for your mortgage advisory business. He shares four varying approaches from brokers operating today.

He then examines the tech needed to simplify the procedure with the sales process concluded.

A blueprint for the Mortgage Adviser and Broker to determine your ideal mortgage and protection advisory sales process.

Your Mortgage Sales Process

The mortgage market is hotting up considerably. Many people enter the sector as brokers or advisers, many working for themselves or for small firms and networks. Gone are the large lender sales forces and, with it, the structured selling processes that dominated.

With the advent of the small operator, everyone can advise in the process of their choice. Naturally, there are regulatory requirements from MCOBs and ICOBS that tend to dominate broker selling processes. Still, you mustn't forget how helpful a sales process can be that contains the steps to undertake, the compliance requirements, the advice and the selling steps.

This chapter will address that need and give you several options for creating your own sales process to operate from. Plus, you can use this to scale your operation if that's what your goal is.

MCOB Regulatory Requirements

It starts with the regulatory requirements that need to be met within your selling steps. Your supervisor will observe you against these mandatory requirements to ensure you stick to them. Remember, there's much more to advising and selling mortgages than regulatory requirements.

Financial Promotion Rules	Advertising and lead generation rules
	Calling Codes of Conduct
Status and Fee Disclosure	Client Agreement and IDD
	Adviser Status
	Services/Costs/Fee Disclosure
Know Your Customer	Vulnerable Customer Recognition
	Affordability and DIP Requirements
	Full Factfind Completion
	Identified Mortgage and Protection Needs
Suitable Advice	Present Suitable Advice
	KFI or ESIS Explained
	Explain Cancellation Rights
	Suitability Letter issued
	On-Going Charges Explained

Supervisor Observation Aids

Typical supervisor observation aids are dominated by the MCOB or ICOB requirements and focus on mandatory covered items.

After all, if you don't deliver the regulatory areas, you are not compliant and can be withdrawn from giving regulated advice. And rightly so too.

More progressive supervisor regimes also develop your other advising, communication, and selling skills. On the next page is an observation aid taken from a brokerage designed to assess an adviser's other skills – or the desirable elements.

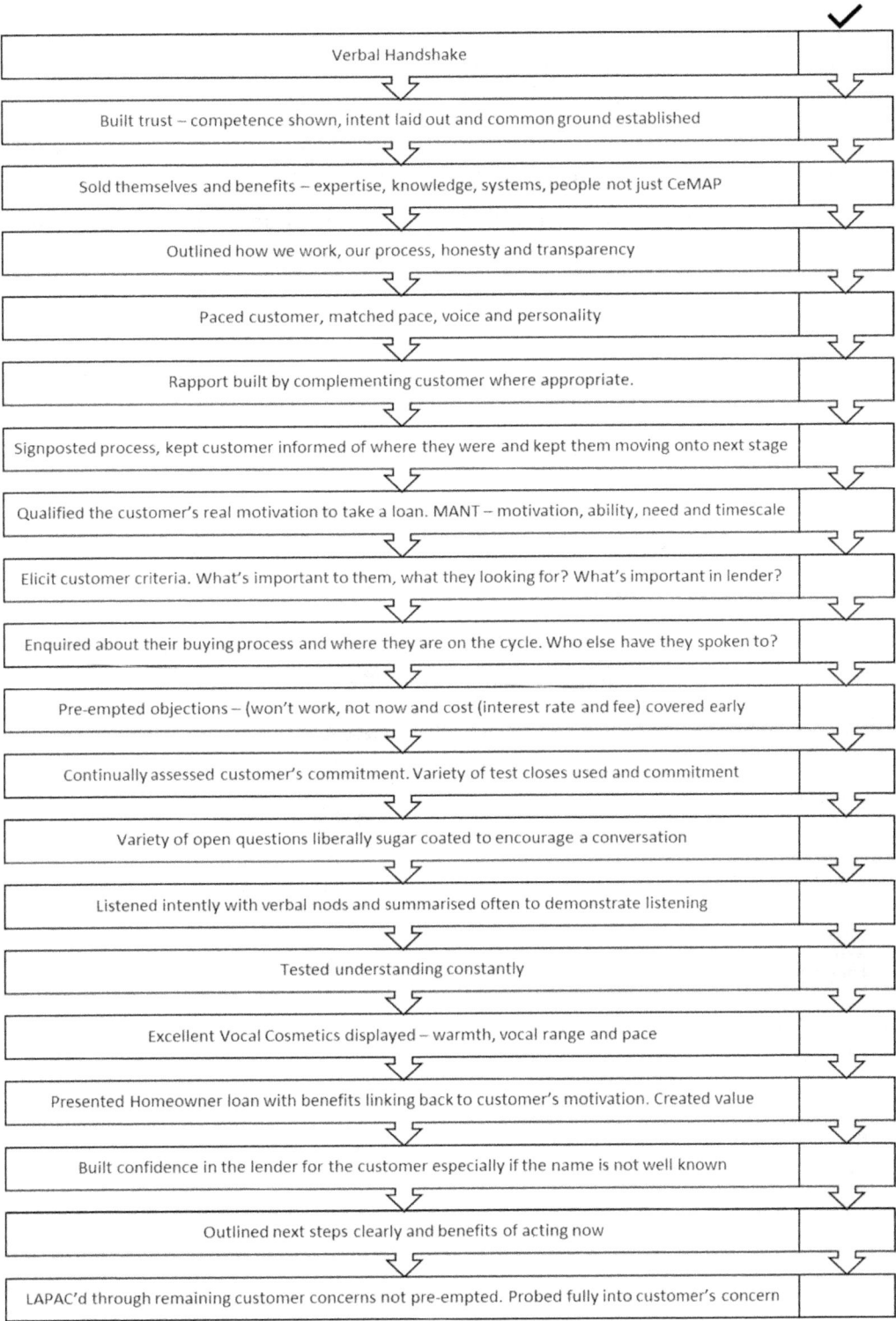

	✓
Verbal Handshake	
Built trust – competence shown, intent laid out and common ground established	
Sold themselves and benefits – expertise, knowledge, systems, people not just CeMAP	
Outlined how we work, our process, honesty and transparency	
Paced customer, matched pace, voice and personality	
Rapport built by complementing customer where appropriate.	
Signposted process, kept customer informed of where they were and kept them moving onto next stage	
Qualified the customer's real motivation to take a loan. MANT – motivation, ability, need and timescale	
Elicit customer criteria. What's important to them, what they looking for? What's important in lender?	
Enquired about their buying process and where they are on the cycle. Who else have they spoken to?	
Pre-empted objections – (won't work, not now and cost (interest rate and fee) covered early	
Continually assessed customer's commitment. Variety of test closes used and commitment	
Variety of open questions liberally sugar coated to encourage a conversation	
Listened intently with verbal nods and summarised often to demonstrate listening	
Tested understanding constantly	
Excellent Vocal Cosmetics displayed – warmth, vocal range and pace	
Presented Homeowner loan with benefits linking back to customer's motivation. Created value	
Built confidence in the lender for the customer especially if the name is not well known	
Outlined next steps clearly and benefits of acting now	
LAPAC'd through remaining customer concerns not pre-empted. Probed fully into customer's concern	

Broker Sales Proceses

The process you use is entirely dependent on how you obtain your leads and the buying process that your customer has been through before they meet you.

Below are four examples from four different advisers/brokers. You can see how their process varies according to obtaining new clients. This is important.

1. The Lending Advice Team gets theirs via branch leads, calls from the website and existing customers.

2. The Directly Authorised Broker gets theirs from referrals, agent leads, bought leads.

3. The Seconds/Bridging Broker gets theirs by buying leads, website incoming calls (all urgent).

4. The New Homes Broker gets theirs by agent leads, New Home Site leads (all urgent).

Corporate Lender Advice Team

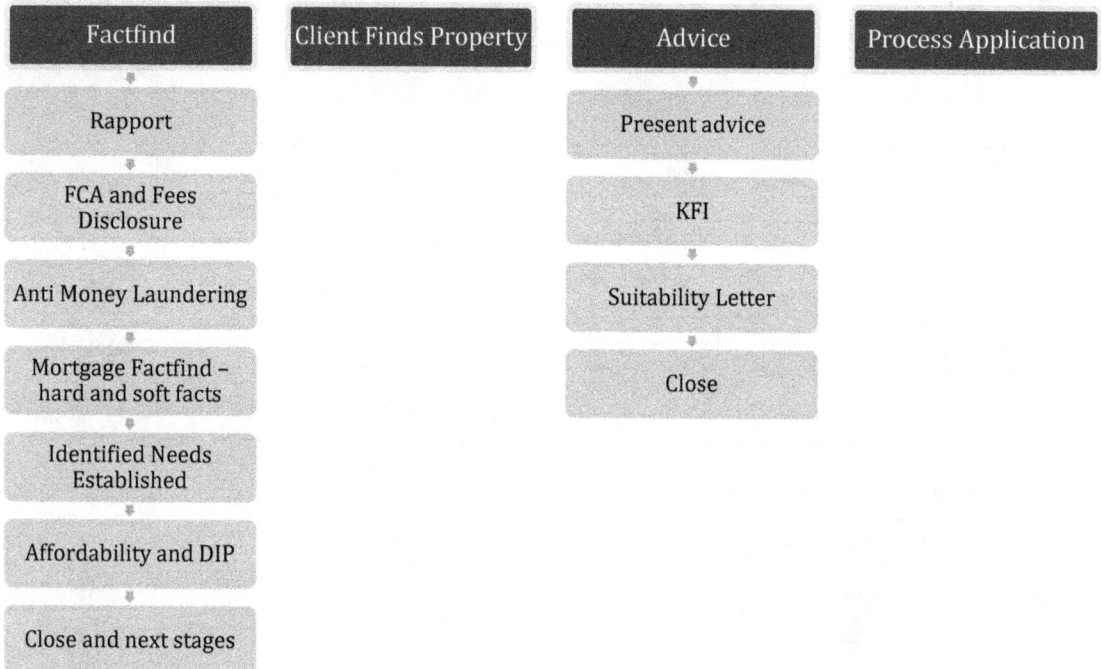

Factfind	Client Finds Property	Advice	Process Application
Rapport		Present advice	
FCA and Fees Disclosure		KFI	
Anti Money Laundering		Suitability Letter	
Mortgage Factfind – hard and soft facts		Close	
Identified Needs Established			
Affordability and DIP			
Close and next stages			

Directly Authorised Broker

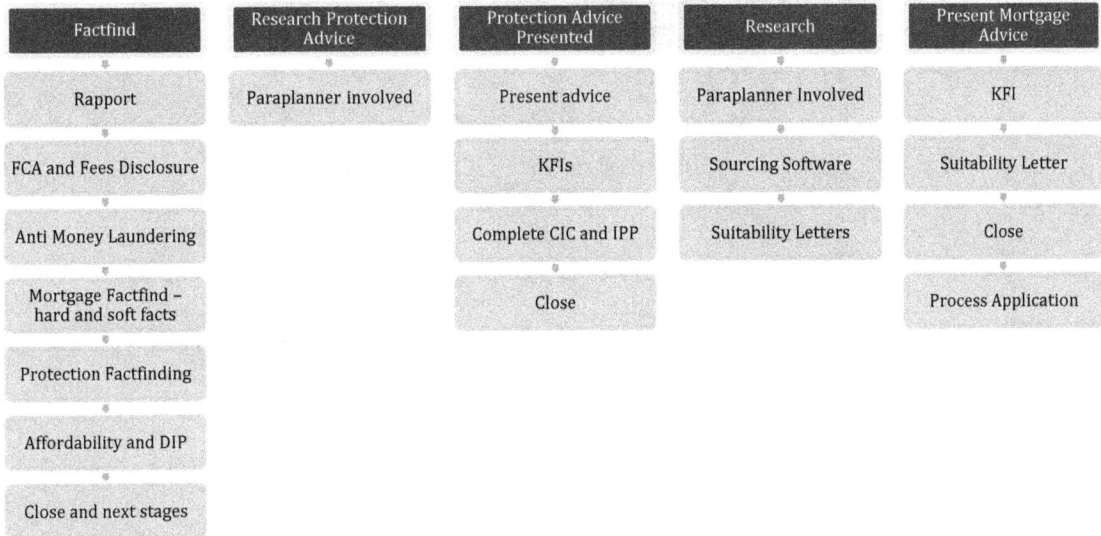

Factfind	Research Protection Advice	Protection Advice Presented	Research	Present Mortgage Advice
Rapport	Paraplanner involved	Present advice	Paraplanner Involved	KFI
FCA and Fees Disclosure		KFIs	Sourcing Software	Suitability Letter
Anti Money Laundering		Complete CIC and IPP	Suitability Letters	Close
Mortgage Factfind – hard and soft facts		Close		Process Application
Protection Factfinding				
Affordability and DIP				
Close and next stages				

Seconds/Bridging Broker

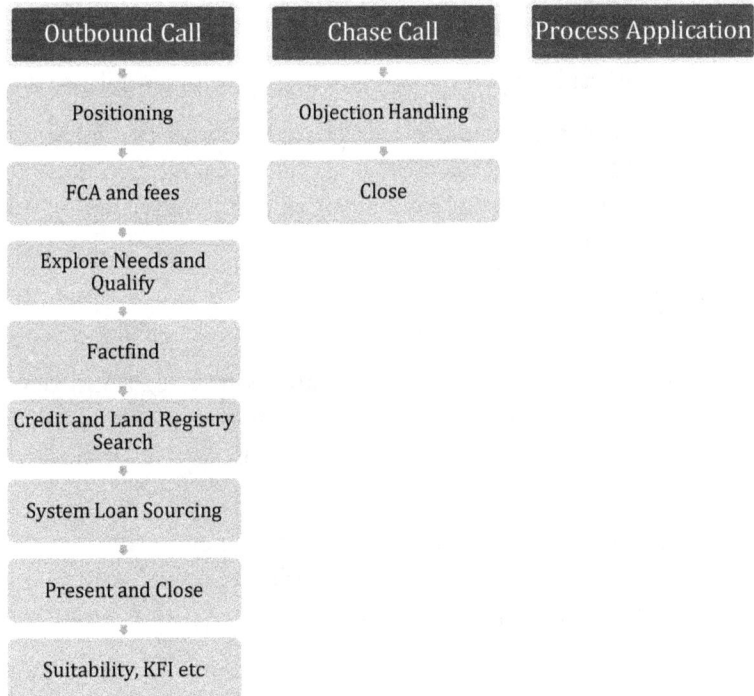

Outbound Call	Chase Call	Process Application
Positioning	Objection Handling	
FCA and fees	Close	
Explore Needs and Qualify		
Factfind		
Credit and Land Registry Search		
System Loan Sourcing		
Present and Close		
Suitability, KFI etc		

New Homes Broker

DIP Call	Factfind	Protection Team
FCA and Qualify Call	Hard and soft facts	Review Factfind
Affordability	Identified Needs Established	Quotes out to Client
Soft Credit Search	Sourcing Software	Follow up call
DIP Issued	Advice given and KFIs	Close on Protection
Report to Builder/Agent	Application Online	Suitability etc
	Suitability Letters	

The 15 Minute Discovery Video Call

This may be new to you, especially if you come from a corporate lender background.

Oddly called an Interview, the first meeting was geared around the factfinding process. It included rapport, trust-building and disclosure but quickly moved to the factfind process. When you're in a traditional lender led environment, and you're advising on a scheme from a restricted range, this worked well.

But when you're in a competitive environment, feeding on internet generated leads, buying leads, referrals and such, starting with a discovery call works very well.

The discovery call allows you to fix a meeting quickly from a lead and doesn't require an enormous commitment from a prospective customer. It enables you to qualify them, assesses their situation and goals, and explain your value before the fee is disclosed and the "time clock" starts.

Mortgage advisers generally don't charge fees; brokers do. They need to promote their value before advising the price. We can talk about costs another day, but suffice it to say, brokers do a whole lot more work than advisers, hence the fee.

The objective for the video discovery call is to proceed to a full factfind if you feel you and the customer wish to do so.

Here are the typical steps of the first 15-minute video discovery call:

Discovery Call

Break the ice

Value proposition

Sow the seed for referrals later on

FCA Authorisation and Status

Discuss customer's overall goals and aims

Qualify the customer and assess where they are in their "buying process."

Build trust, gauge their personality

Discuss next steps and fee disclosure

Gain agreement to proceed

The Fee Conversation

Within the first 15-minute discovery call comes the fee conversation. If you charge a fee, this needs disclosing, but there is an order to do this, covered in the first 15 minutes.

The Fee Conversation

↓

Have the correct State of Mind – work on your Inner Game

↓

Deliver your Value Proposition – who you are, how you work, who you work with and your value.

↓

FCA Authorisation – confirms your professional standing as a regulated adviser

↓

Contextualise with other professionals in the house buying process – lawyers, surveyors, accountants – and the fees they charge

↓

Introduce your fee and the value you deliver for this

↓

Gain commitment

↓

Disclosure documentation.

Tech to Improve the Sales Process

Tech dominates, and so it should too. Progressive advisers and brokers use tech to enhance the customer experience, speed up processes and generally add to the value they provide.

Here are some examples of current tech used by brokers:

- Lead generation sites such as leadpronto, theleadengine and leadsbridge will, for a fee, provide you with internet generated leads to fertilise your business.

- CRM – Customer Relationship Manager software helps you collect client contact data, provide a history of activity, and move the customer along your sales process. Simple systems such as Capsule or MS Dynamics can assist here. Still, many networks and adviser firms have their own bespoke client software that integrates everything.

- Email and Calendar software – again, this is often incorporated within your CRM. Still, a standalone system such as MS 365 will work well.

- Advice software is highly bespoke, allowing you to capture client details on a factfind, link to the sourcing engines and produce all the regulatory paperwork such as a suitability letter. Iress is a market leader delivering the Xplan range.

- Sourcing software allows you to search the market for loans and select a suitable mortgage for the client. Mortgage Brain, Trigold, L&Gs SmartrCriteria all work well

- Life Assurance and GI sourcing allows you to do the same but with protection plans

- DIP engines allow you to link to lender's Agreement in Principle (AIP) apps and approve or assess how much a client can borrow and what scheme to suit.

- Client review and testimonial sites such as unbiased, vouchedfor or Trustpilot are essential these days.

Summary

A contentious subject. Some brokers prefer to stick to the regulated steps and flow with everything else. That's fine if you're very experienced and like to freewheel. If you want more structure and are looking to scale your business with more advice, you need a structured approach.

Suppose you want to take coaching and mentoring seriously by developing your advisers. In that case, you need a sales process to coach them, help them improve their skills in working the process and give clients first-class advice on their mortgage and protection needs.

To Fee or Not to Fee

Chapter Summary

Professional advisers, consultants, and experts – anyone who gives advice on a specialist topic or subject charges fees. I've been charging fees since setting out on my own 21 years ago. Still, the purpose of this chapter is to help those new to fee-charging so you don't repeat the mistakes of those professionals who started charging fees way before you.

Should You Charge a Fee?

If your advice is worth paying for, then yes. If it's not, then no.

Why do we charge a fee compared with taking a commission or receiving remuneration from the products and services we advise?

Some of us have been forced to by our regulator; it provides a regular source of income, creates committed and qualified clients, and has fewer conflict of interest discussions.

It enhances our image as professional consultants and allows us to be treated alongside our peers in the profession. It permits you to be rewarded for the value you put in, not just for the hours you toil, with fees the client values your advice more since they have put a monetary value on it and fees are demanded by clients who don't see you as a commodity or a product pusher and don't want any conflict of interest.

Adviser reticence can occasionally spoil the broth.

Why are we reticent then?

Many advisers are not; my research shows that many advisers handle fees expertly, but some do not.

Much of it is nervousness about the value/fee relationship, caginess in case the client starts to negotiate or push back on your fee.

It's this procrastination to enter into a discussion about their fees at an early stage of the relationship that sours the trust and generates future wariness on the part of the adviser.

But much of it is in the head.

The Inner Game Battle – Knowing Your Value

The Inner Game is a term that relates to what goes on inside our heads, our motivation, drive and state of mind when handling ourselves with clients.

The first step in mastering how to handle fees is to convince yourself that your fee is right, justified, and a valid reward for the value you are to provide for your client. My research shows that some advisers have anxieties over their fee – they believe it's too much or too little and doesn't represent the value they provide.

The secret is to have confidence in the value you provide, to believe in this value yourself, to buy the value if you were in the market for the same.

In their book Competing on Value, Hanan and Karp talk about "knowing your value, price your value and sell your value".

Without putting any more gloss on the topic, that's the secret. Suppose you believe in the value and service you provide and can articulate it clearly. In that case, your fee will be received favourably, and your client will not argue the matter with you.

You need to believe in your value proposition and have this written down briefly so that it distinguishes you perfectly from others in your profession.

So how can we verbalise our value proposition?

The 7 Questions to Ask Yourself to Know Your Value

Ask yourself the following 7 questions:

1. Who am I?
2. What do I do?
3. Why do I do what I do?
4. How do I do what I do?
5. Who have I performed services for?
6. What makes me different from other advisers?
7. Why should clients do business with me?

Have a trusted friend ask you the questions in a coaching style, audio record the answers you give and transcribe these into a value proposition or elevator pitch or sound bite. It doesn't matter what you call it; just get it clear, concise and valuable.

Then carry out some belief change work if you still don't believe in your value. You simply have to be your own number one fan whatever we do.

With your Inner Game settled in your head, let's look at how experienced and successful advisers handle the fee issue with clients. Firstly we need to head back to the most fundamental requirement of any adviser/client relationship – trust.

Trust – Fundamentally Has to Be There

We know that, don't we? We looked at the topic in the previous chapter, but do you remember that trust is built from three elements. Your clients will instinctively look for these before they learn to trust you.

They are your competence in knowing what you're doing, your intentions and ethics and finally, your empathy and ability to connect with them as a human being.

Rather obvious but worth highlighting. Here are a few new takes on the three elements to consider.

Competence

Your competence comes over time and is probably something you've gained over years of study and experience. Don't assume the client knows you're competent. Don't brag but focus on showing them that you are a safe pair of hands.

Explaining things simply and clearly has been recognised as the best method of proving your competence.

It's easy to make something simple complicated, but it's very skilful at making something complex appear simple. That's the mark of competence.

The other point about competence is the impact of the team around you. Approximately 20% of your client's contact will be with you; 80% will be with your support team. So do they demonstrate competence? Exams are one thing; relating and explaining things is another.

Empathy

Empathy and relationship building is for another day, intentions and ethics link straight to the fees handling the issue, so we need to secure this.

Ethics and Intentions

Ethics are how you do things naturally, honesty, trustworthiness. All essentials.

Your reputation, your brand comes in here – your underlying intentions are key. The problem is that not handling the fee issue can cause terminal damage to how your client sees your intentions; they'll begin to see a chink in your integrity if we gloss over fees, procrastinate and put off the conversation.

Being up-front and clear, very transparent about your fee structure builds trust. Not being clear can damage irrevocably the relationship you need.

Openness and transparency are essential.

So how do we make sure we do this?

The 4 Underlying Principles When Discussing Fees

I've mentioned the word a few times already – procrastination.

Don't Procrastinate

The first principle is not to avoid the issue. It's quickly done, and I've seen it with many advisers. They're worried about the outcome, so put it off to the end of the meeting, and that's wrong.

The surgeon who has bad news for the patient is not going to put off telling you. He won't enjoy the process, but he'll sit you down and explain clearly and slowly, outlying the various options available.

I'm not saying we should compare our service with operating on a human being. Still, the key is how the surgeon handles this tricky issue.

Just do it, don't linger, as there's a price to pay in trust if you don't.

Clarity

The second principle is clarity. The surgeon speaks clearly and succinctly, so should we. Have a simple fee tariff, easy to explain and understand.

Don't confuse the issue with science, be clear and precise. Give headline information and let the client delve deeper if they wish.

Provide a Context

The third principle is to provide a context with your fee. Help them see how the market sets the cost and where your price fits. It might be higher or lower; that's your choice, but explain why this is so.

When I buy a car, I know what it should cost; Glass's Guide helps me, and the internet is fabulous at making costs transparent. This is a commodity; you're not.

Fee Reinforcement

Finally, help the client refer to the documentation that outlines your fee as clearly as possible. Don't surround this with excess detail. All clients like to reflect after the meeting, and having something to refer to afterwards is essential.

How To Go About It?

You need a process to follow, a way of working that suits your environment and style, then stick to this process.

Early in the meeting, you need to introduce yourself, how you work and most importantly, your value proposition. Remember, it's your value that justifies the fee.

Then talk about the fee with confidence and self-assuredness. You're worth it, as the TV ad goes.

Many successful advisers link this into only having a certain number of clients, so their time can be allocated accordingly, thus giving value to the client.

Other advisers have allied this conversation to running their referral only business. Because my business grows by clients referring their friends and associates, I ensure that they receive the maximum value possible – I need to earn your referrals first with my value and service.

It's all about words and confidence in what you do and the value you provide. Clients expect to be charged a fee for professional advice and want this to be made apparent upfront by a confident adviser who can articulate clearly the service they provide.

That's really all there is to it.

The "How Much Can I Borrow" Meeting

Chapter Summary

A plan for holding the affordability meeting with your clients, helping them understand what they can borrow, the costs and "locking" them into using you.

An important meeting is often sandwiched between disclosure and factfinding but crucial. Valuable to ensure your client can afford the mortgage, gives them the confidence to start house hunting and is essential for trust-building.

It's also pretty handy at qualifying the customer if they've been referred by an agent or builder.

This chapter will share all you need to know to run highly-effective meetings.

Why a Separate Conversation?

In the autumn of 1988, I'd just left a safe Building Society Manager job to foray as a Mortgage Adviser for an estate agency chain. In the Building Society, the role was pretty easy. It was all about advising and helping customers who wanted to deal with us for their mortgage.

In the agency environment, it was very different. Highly competitive, pretty ruthless and eye-watering targets. It was my first month, and I wasn't doing exceptionally well. The double tax relief had ended the previous month, and the housing market was a bubble about to go bang. The business was scarce.

In walked the couple; they had offered one of our properties and were keen to process their mortgage with me. Hooray, some business. After a long meeting on affordability and factfinding, I recommended a mortgage with the Britannia Building Society. Along with an endowment with my firm, the Prudential.

The meeting was long, and all that was needed was to complete the application form, so I gave it to the couple to complete and return to me after the weekend.

A big mistake, as it happened.

A few days later, nothing, so I phoned them, and they said they had dropped it off at the Britannia branch in the High Street.

I'd lost the case. How? Because I hadn't been sharp enough to gain commitment and process the matter myself. Boy, did I learn from that blunder?

In the same way, when you're helping the client with their "How much can I borrow" question, make sure you gain commitment and move them onto the next stage. Otherwise, you'll be working for free, and they'll go elsewhere. A few subtle changes can make all the difference. Let me explain how.

Purpose and Structure of the Meeting

The purpose of the meeting is to prepare the client. To help them understand what the house purchase and sale will cost, their monthly repayments and the amount of mortgage you can arrange for them.

Naturally, most clients will know this when they are offering on a property. This meeting is typically carried out earlier in the process when they have just begun their house search.

It's also why it's a dangerous meeting since you can arm the client with lots of helpful information and ideas. They will be confronted with lots of eager mortgage advisers during their home odyssey.

So an element of commitment and influence is needed on your part.

Here's a typical structure that I've seen working well from countless mortgage brokers.

Affordability and DIP

Summarise client goals

Consulting on the costs of buying and selling

Current Income and Expenditure conversation

Budget discussion

Affordability and maximum mortgage software

Credit Report discussion

Official DIP Issued

Gain commitment for next stage

Benefits of the Affordability Meeting

There are many benefits of helping your client with this meeting. Here are a few that come to mind:

- Proves competence and builds trust.
- Educates clients on how to "fix" their affordability, e.g. credit file, loans etc.
- Ideal for handling professional referrals, i.e. estate agents, new homes.
- Qualifies client for loan etc.
- Arms client with all financial details.
- "Locks" clients in to use you when they are ready to proceed, i.e. found.
- Sows the seed for package and protection.
- Creates budget.
- Logical step.
- Utilise video capabilities, sharing whiteboards, websites etc.
- Compliance aspects such as AML dealt with and essential paperwork curated for later submission.

Preparing the Client for the Meeting

Education, Education, Education

Tony Blair was reported to say this during a Labour party conference. He drove home the need to educate the country's youngsters. He was true to his word too.

Mortgage advisers educate clients during the various meetings we conduct beforehand. Mortgage clients nowadays like to do their research before they meet you. They have a limitless internet library to help them do this, and many brokers provide content for them to consume.

This can be counterproductive for you because they might stagger onto another broker's web presence. Gorge on the education pieces and use that broker to arrange their mortgage.

Before your meeting is scheduled, invite them to view, read or listen to your material. Which has your stamp on it and your spin. Brokers record podcasts to listen to; there are some outstanding ones out there on Spotify. Write articles and publish them on your website. Seriously consider a YouTube Channel where you can house your video collection full of educational material for your clients.

Once your assets are created, you can place them on your favourite social media where your clients "hang out". Facebook, LinkedIn, Instagram, YouTube and so on.

This is very time-consuming, and you may not have the space to do this. I get it. If that's the case, turn to the curation of assets, not creation. Carefully curate your own material from selected resources that aren't linked to broker competition. Government websites such as the Money Advice Service. The Land Registry, Martin Lewis' site, "Which", and so on can all give valuable and reliable information. They may not have adverts for other brokers.

To Portal or Not to Portal, That is the Question

With clients, plenty of attention is spent just collecting information from them. It's pretty dull, uninspiring and just data. Some brokers encourage the clients to pre-fill their data capture form on a website. A portal of some description.

The client spends 25 minutes, at home, on their laptop, just filling in a form telling you all about themselves.

This has lots of advantages for you and your client. It saves time for you both to allow more discussion and questions in the meeting. It builds commitment in that the client invests their time and probably won't want to do this again. You can simply pre-populate your factfind or questionnaire at a flick of a switch. The data is accurate since the client completed it.

However, some clients just don't find the time to do it, promise faithfully they will. But never get around to it and swear the login codes you gave them didn't work, or they never received the email. Don't take it personally. It's just people.

Homework for Your Client

If the portal request falls on death ears, you need to influence the client to do easy homework. Influencing requires benefits to encourage action. Whatever your request, give a reason and benefit. The client will more than likely adhere to your request.

Putting together a portfolio of documents on PDF is essential. Occasionally, lenders may ask for paper copies of various items, but most accept PDFs that you can easily upload. Clients can simply photo documents using their phones and convert them to PDF before emailing them to you. Some advisers use WhatsApp or other messaging services to easily transport PDF documents.

Here's an extensive hairy list:

- A form of ID such as your driving licence or passport.

- Your last 3 years address history with no gaps.

- Your most recent monthly payslips and P60.

- Your last 3 months' bank statements.

- Details for credit cards, loans, or hire purchase agreements you have.

- Details of any insurance policies, e.g., home insurance, mortgage payment protection, life or critical illness cover.

- Details of any Benefits in Kind from your employer.

- Accountant's Certificate; or your last 2 years' accounts; or tax calculations (SA302s) plus Tax Year Overviews (TYOs) covering your previous 2 years.

- Copy of contract and evidence of your income, e.g., payslips.

- Overtime/bonus/commission.

- If your overtime/bonus/commission is annual - your P60s from the last 3 years.

Getting Your Client "Mortgage Ready"

I would run a decidedly old car that constantly needed repair in my youth. I would be under the bonnet most Sunday mornings, tweaking the spark plugs and points to start on Monday morning. I used to dread the annual MOT. A negative mark would mean the bus or train to my workplace, so I prepared as much to make sure my car was MOT ready.

In the same way, you can educate your client to get themselves "mortgage ready".

The MOT test was transparent. If you knew where to look, you could determine what the mechanics would assess your car against. Tyre treads, windscreen wipers, exhaust pipe "blowing",, lights and bulbs.

All routine checks only require a visit to Halfords.

Here are some areas your client can prepare themselves to be "mortgage ready":

Self Employed

Self-employed clients need to be prepared more than ever before. The pandemic didn't treat self-employed too well; some struggled and are only just repairing their finances. Many benefitted from the lockdown, for example, builders and tradespeople. As a result, lenders are wary but not preventative.

Self-employed and owner-directors need to ensure their accounts are in good shape. SA302s can be obtained directly from HMRC's website, and lenders love these documents. Any bounce back loans can be repaid or shown in the accounts that benefited the business rather than paid their salaries for months.

Contractors

Contractors or those on fixed-term durations have been hammered by IR35. As a result, some have migrated back to employed status, which are favourites for lenders. Someone on a fixed-term contract is inherently risky. Still, suppose you can demonstrate a seamless transition from contract to contract, a history of work. In that case, a lender will view this positively.

Loans

Loans, credit cards and other mandatory expenditures will damage your affordability as well as your credit file. Can any of these loans be repaid from equity in the current home? Could credit cards be refunded before the mortgage is applied? Can you reduce the lease cost of your brand-new car by limiting your annual mileage? These will all help affordability.

Statements

Bank statements, P60s, and so on all need to be accessed. Printed bank statements are a legacy of the past since we all use Smartphone Apps. Clients can access statements via the desktop apps as PDFs or, at the significantly worse, trot down to the branch (if it's still open) and ask branch staff to print them off for you.

They will.

Credit Score

Finally, your credit score. There are plenty of resources your client can access with advice on how to improve your credit score. Careful they don't go snooping around a competitor's guide. Your client trusts you to provide your own guidance rather than referring them to another website. Initially, they need to be aware of their score.

The best venue is checkmyfile.com, where a 30-day free period will allow your client to access their score from the major credit search sites. These are Experian, Equifax and Transunion. 99.9% of your lenders will use one or all of these firms.

Here are some ways you can improve your score:

- Make sure you appear on the electoral roll at your current address.

- Ensure your current address is correct on all of your accounts.

- If you have any existing credit agreements, stay within 50% of your available credit amount.

- Make complete and timely payments on all accounts held in your name.

- If you have a low score due to a lack of credit, special credit builder credit cards can be helpful.

- Use a credit card and pay off your credit cards regularly and on time.

- Pay your bills via direct debit.

- Tidy up old bank accounts.

- Avoid using your overdraft.

- Use Experian Boost – so that your Netflix, Spotify, Council Tax payments and other payments can boost your score.

- Un-link yourself from ex-partners (you might not realise you are still financially connected).

Eventually, I moved into a mortgage adviser role that gave me a company car. The dreaded MOT no longer gave me sleepless nights.

Consulting on Costs

Depending on how the client arrived at your doorstep will decide whether they are familiar with the costs involved in buying and selling. They may be a remortgage client or a professional landlord, which will also influence how much they already know.

However, they need to be aware of the costs and have some capital put aside to pay them or will be allocating some of their equity.

Running through the costs involved lends itself perfectly to the video model. If you're using Zoom or Teams, sharing screens is a straightforward and powerful way of engaging your client.

Have websites open and ready to illustrate the costs. Here are some sites and the prices involved:

- Moneyed.co.uk has an intelligent template for you to use with your client that works out the costs. It is a non-lender or competitor, so ideal. One of the critical aspects of the affordability conversation with clients is not to pin them on a particular lender.

- Land Registry.

- Gov.co.uk with Stamp Duty, Capital Gains Tax etc.

- Surveyor sites for information about the main types of surveys and costs.

- A local solicitor for the legal fees.

- Environmental search information such as the Coal Board.

A tip for you. It's always a good idea to reflect the client on other professionals in the buying and selling process who charge fees. Some relatively high too that reflect their time spent on the case. Lawyers come to mind, of course, surveyors and accountants. Even estate agents. When you cement your own fee, have these costs in the client's mind. You're a professional and should charge fees for your service too.

Don't let the proc fee undermine your value. After all, procs fees are not guaranteed to continue at their level. History has witnessed these to be somewhat fragile and at the whim of lenders who only pay them when they need intermediaries to lend their money. When they can lend their money themselves, they don't need you. Just beware; history repeats itself.

The Income and Expenditure Conversation

Use the shared screen at this point. Find an online calculator; there are hundreds to gather the information. If your client has pre-populated this information, give yourself a house point because this is quite a mundane and dreary process, asking how much they spend etc.

You're not going to input the totals into an Agreement in Principle engine yet. That will come next. This part of the meeting allows you to educate the client on the expenditure and affordability. Knowledge of the affordability process is essential here. I'll remind you of this shortly. But first, let's hammer home the budget question.

Right now is a perfect spot to find out the budget for the mortgage payments. Earlier, when you introduced yourself and how you work – your value proposition – you clearly described how you work. Your calling, your professional responsibility is to ensure that all your clients can afford their mortgage commitments but also afford to protect the mortgage from any peril that can jeopardise ownership. Death, long term illness, critical illness, fire, flooding – the list goes on.

Now is the time to elicit the budget. An estimate of how much your client can reasonably afford to pay for all of this.

Relate it to the rent if they're first-time buyers. Link it to the earlier mortgage they've had. Convey protection costs to car insurance if you have to.

Keep this budget an estimate and promise that you'll be looking at lender specific payments shortly.

You'll source the best possible scheme to fit their needs when applying for a mortgage.

What's Under the Bonnet of an AIP?

2014 witnessed the Mortgage Market Review. The regulator's knee jerk reaction to the causes of the financial crash, which occurred just 6 years earlier. It tightened affordability rules and rid lenders of their love of multipliers of income, which they had cherished for many years.

It brought tight affordability guidelines and based payments around a stressed interest rate rather than the current ultra-low one.

Lenders reacted by applying tech to the problem. A spreadsheet is put into an app. So every lender has their Decision in Principle or DIP engine online, which you use to find out how much they are willing to lend a client.

Not difficult.

But what's under the bonnet?

Income comes first. Profits, salary, bonuses etc

Less expenditure of the client:

- Mandatory expenditure such as loans and credit cards. Existing mortgage payments that are not being repaid. Anything that is contracted.

- Cost of living spending. Many engines use government statistics for average expenditure for typical families. The Office of National Statistics (ONS) provides this.

- Discretionary spending can affect some DIPs, but the ONS figures will pick this up.

This gives Net Disposable Income (NDI) in which lenders will use to decide how much of a monthly payment for the mortgage this will buy. Typically, they will allow 80% of this to match the monthly payment.

The monthly payment this NDI matches is the amount at the stressed rate, typically 4 or 5 % above the charging rate. This reflects their view of where rates may rise and whether the client can afford the increased payments.

Affordability Engine Input

As earlier, a marvellous opportunity now to let tech do some heavy lifting. Shared screens on video can be engaging and involving for the client.

The secret sauce here is to not put all your eggs in one basket, so to speak. You mustn't pigeonhole your client onto any specific lender. They may not have found a home yet, so your advantage of being Whole of Market will be eroded with time. Rates change, deals come in at the last moment, and fixed-rate money comes and goes.

Ensure the client knows this and your capability.

Use a specific lender's Decision in Principle (DIP) engine if you wish. They all have them. You'll have to at some stage before you submit the application anyway. I prefer a generic one. The government's Money Advice Service have an excellent example at moneyhelper.org.uk. Just search for their mortgage affordability calculator. It's clear, visual and quickly shared online with your client.

Locking in Your Client

Allow me the embarrassment of revisiting my story from earlier. My failure with the client was not gaining commitment or "locking" them into me. They innocently popped into Britannia's local branch to drop off the application. They didn't think about how it affected me. My mistake.

So think of ways to ensure your client uses you to complete the mortgage application when they find their home. At the very least, just ask them. Use a phrase that merely asks that they're happy to go ahead with you when they have found it. Get their commitment. It's not rocket science to just ask them. You don't need any fancy words or 1990's closing techniques unless you wish to. Just find a casual way of asking them to call back when they are ready to proceed.

Ideas to Lock-In

- Confirm with the client that they really don't want or need to go through this preparation again.

- Use the sympathy vote. I've already invested time with you; I'm sure you feel you want to return that favour and come back to me when you've found it.

- Charge a fee after the 15 Minute Discovery Call, so the client is already "on the clock."

- Just assume with your language that they'll be returning.

- Make it crystal clear that the choice of lender will occur when they've found so getting the best deal possible is open to them via you.

- Start the application in some way to ensure you both save time and lock them in. Protection could be started, a medical questionnaire or proposal. Naturally, you would have done some factfinding at this point.

- Signpost the client to the actual next steps in your process. Book a meeting to conduct the factfind online. Depending on the situation, you may be moving straight onto this next stage anyway.

- Issue a DIP that confirmed their mortgage capability. After all, this was the main benefit or outcome of the meeting as far as the client is concerned. Make them aware this is not a "done deal". However, the DIP is vastly influential at putting others off the scent as the client finds their ideal home.

They will encounter some very sharp sales persuasion techniques on their travels. Methods that shouldn't really be allowed, but home hunting is fraught with emotions and clients can be susceptible to tactics from others.

Make sure they aren't. I wish I had done that all those years ago.

Conversational Factfinding Skills

How to have a Conversational Factfind

If you're in the business of giving mortgage advice, you know that it's tightly regulated to ensure the customer is advised on the most appropriate solution based upon their needs. And that's the absolutely right thing to do.

The problem is that firms and individuals who are tasked with this "advice risk" don't want to get it wrong and be sued later with a visit from the Financial Ombudsman Service. So they've tightened the process almost to the extent of scripting questions to ask.

The consequence is a torrid experience for the poor old customer. Not all, but a good 50% of mortgage factfinds are stifling, scripted and interrogative. I kid you not. They've been structured by risk-averse compliance people who are genuinely interviewed. The irony is that they don't have to be so.

Hard Fact Conversation

Factfinding consists of several areas. Many hard facts about the customer and softer information comprise criteria and preferences. We'll start with the pure facts.

These are straightforward to obtain. Most factfinds contain boxes for which you ask the appropriate question, and then you fill them in. These are great on a screen because they're used to populate your advice system, application forms and suitability reports, so it saves a whole lotta time.

We want a conversation, not an interrogation or question and answer session. Many advisers are taught open versus closed and sugar-coating techniques to ask more pleasant questions. They have first-class listening and empathy skills to keep the customer talking. However, it's still a question and answers session, albeit an agreeable one.

You need to use my Conversation Cycle technique to create an authentic conversation. Allow me to explain.

The Conversation Cycle

A typical questioning session involves person A asking the question, person B answering it, person A following up with another question and person B answering. Nothing wrong with that approach, but it isn't a conversation. Conversations swing back and forth and can continue for ages. Let's mash this up a bit.

Person A still asks a question. You can do all the sugar coating and softening you like with this question, make it a high gain, curious, open question if you want, and person B still answers it. But this time, person A does some form of acknowledging to encourage more response from person B.

This can be:

A verbal nod such as "I see", "That's fascinating", or "Keep going".

An empathy statement that shows you've experienced just the same thing. A "me too" moment. For example, person B might answer the question about their holiday in Florida when they swam with the dolphins. Person A would empathise with, "We holidayed in Florida last year, and the weather was fantastic, but we didn't get to that theme park. It sounds fun."

A reflective statement such as "Swimming with dolphins must have been an amazing experience".

Now, these acknowledgements turn things around immensely. The aim is to allow person B to talk, and conversation can ensue quite quickly. But let me finish off the cycle in style for you and add a fourth element.

So person A asks a question, person B is kind enough to respond, person A then throws in an acknowledgement, person B doesn't respond. Hence, person A throws in an "inform".

An "inform" is merely a statement, a precursor to another question. Some new context to launch the next phase of the conversation. It allows you to steer the conversation in the direction you seek. For example, following our dolphin story.

Person A might acknowledge and say how fascinating that must have been and might add, "Holidays are an important expenditure for us all, and many clients spend a fair proportion of their disposable income on leisure and holidays".

That's the inform – the context to launch another question such as "What proportion of your disposable income do you like to allocate to leisure activities?"

So that's the cycle:

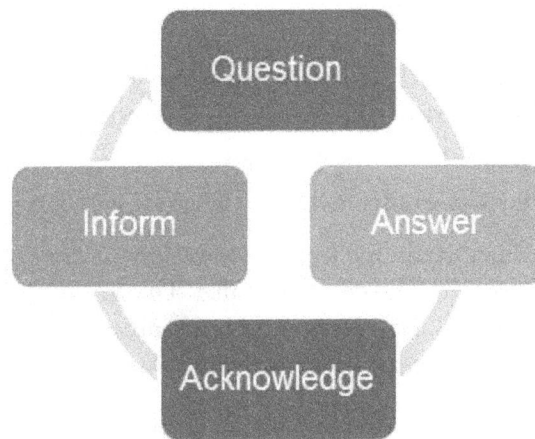

And you can go back and forth, sideways, around the cycle…there are no rules on that; just enjoy a good conversation rather than an interrogation.

Back to Hard Facts

If we apply this technique to gathering hard facts, you can see how it begins to work. Let's role-play the part when the mortgage adviser collects information about the customer's current job role.

"Let's get into the subject of your current job, Mr Khan if that's OK? Tell me about where you currently work?"

Our adviser uses verbal nods as the customer speaks. "OK, I'm with you, that sounds interesting, I bet that's difficult" and so on.

The customer gives more information, and the adviser populates his factfind as he speaks because he's good at that. The customer stops talking.

Our adviser comes in with an "inform". "Your company sounds large enough to have a good company pension scheme. Could you please shed some light on that?"

And the customer continues and mentions his retirement date set by his scheme.

"Ah, so retiring at age 65 means you can put your feet up once and for all. How important is that to have all your debts paid off by then, including your mortgage?"

We've now picked up on some criteria information, so we're testing it to see if we can arrive at some identified needs for the mortgage term.

The moral here is that if you are merely gathering hard facts, listen out for clues that can help you pick soft criteria and needs.

Soft Facts and Mortgage Criteria

We step into the mortgage needs section to elicit the criteria or identified needs to give advice. There are several need areas that advisers ask – term of the loan, budget, risk nature of the mortgage, concerns over interest rates, etc.

Use the conversation cycle in precisely the same way. Let's hit on the term issue again.

Advisers start with, "The State Retirement Age is currently 68 for you, Mr Khan. When were you thinking of giving up work?" The customer talks. The adviser continues, "That's exciting for you. I've got over 30 years before I can stop work unless they bring in robots to do my job. Many of our customers like to have their mortgages repaid as quickly as possible. Where do you stand on this?"

Mr Khan gives information that he wants it paid off as quickly as possible. So the adviser comes in with, "Paying the mortgage off early sounds like a fab goal Mr Khan, but what budget were you looking at putting on the mortgage payments for you to be able to pay it off as soon as you can?"

This will now give you the identified needs to recommend a term.

Let's now take a look at a risk and mortgage repayment method. "Mr Khan, there are broadly two ways in which you can arrange payments on your mortgage. How aware are you of these two methods?" Mr Khan is unsure. "Would you like me to explain them?" And he does. "Which do you find you're pointing towards?" Mr Khan likes the capital and interest. "Yes, capital and interest are popular because you're certain to repay the mortgage at the end of the term, and there are no surprises. So, the certainty of paying is important, is that right, Mr Khan?"

"Certainty of repaying the loan is one thing Mr Khan, and this can also relate to the interest rate on your mortgage, which can impact your attitude as well. There are a variety of mortgage interest types we have available. Have you done any research on these?" Mr Khan says he's looked at the fixed rate and likes this. "Yes, fixed-rate mortgages have many advantages over the others. May I ask Mr Khan, what's steered you towards these?" And he tells you he likes to have control and know his payments; it lets him budget. "I applaud you for that; it's so important to have control over your finances, especially when your home is at risk. Mr Khan, am I hearing that control and stability are vital for you here?"

And bingo, you have another identified need for a mortgage with bulletproof evidence why Mr Khan is suitable for that. Another way to do the mortgage type piece is to come in and inform him of the various types.

"Mr Khan, you're aware I'm sure that we have lots of different types of mortgage on offer here at ABC Bank. How familiar with them are you?" "That's fine, lots of my customers like me to explain them, will you let me do that for you?" So the adviser explains the different types. And every now and then, he pauses and asks for Mr Khan's feelings on it. "So, how do they sound so far? What do you like about them so far?"

"Give me your thoughts, please, Mr Khan?"

"I see; fixed sounds good. Do you mind me asking exactly why?"

And bingo, you have an identified need all within a lively, enjoyable conversation.

Budget again. "Mr Khan, I recall that you like to have a firm grip on your finances. Many customers have a budget in mind that they don't want to exceed. Where do you stand on this?"

And you continue in the same vein.

Believe me, no animals or humans were injured in the making of this movie.

Handling Mortgage Objections - The Modern Way

Chapter Summary

Paul shares how he learnt how to handle customer concerns correctly that didn't cause resentment and combativeness. Paul shows how you can use this technique when talking to your reticent customers.

With empathy, structure and focussed customer concern and service. It's not a battle like it was in the 1990s; now, we're helping the customer decide.

The Market Collapsed

My first foray into mortgage and insurance sales was in late 1988, just as the double tax relief loophole ended. The property market fell over a cliff, and I sat in an estate agency branch twiddling my thumbs. My new employers promised me the earth. Leads, by the hundreds, that you can convert in an instance. I guess before that fateful August, it was like that, but the market had since just comatose and died.

I needed to earn a living, and the agency branch I was based in was desperate for some profits, so I turned to a pal I'd met a few years before at a company called Manufacturers Life. He was a grizzled, life assurance salesman of old—sharp suits, snazzy ties, every inch the successful man. Love him or hate him now; he came to my rescue.

He taught me how to make calls to the extensive database of customers that the agency had. A bristling database of customers garnered over the previous 20 years until they sold out to the giant insurance company that owned the firm I was working for. There were dozens of old box files containing the database, nothing digital to be seen, just reams of sales documents containing the most valuable asset I could want. A name, phone number, and service they had gleefully purchased from us in the last few years. A happy customer.

My reason to call them was a good old fashioned customer service appointment down at the agency office where we would review their situation as part of the ongoing customer support we provided. It was enticing and compelling, and I knew they would benefit from it. And it would keep me busy too.

The Challenge

The challenge I had was to hone my calling script to entice them into my office to chat things through with them. People throw up what I call a "knee jerk reaction". It was an instant rejection because they hadn't had time to think it through and needed to buy time.

Nowadays, we call these customer objections or reservations. A customer said "not now" because they didn't know what else to say back then.

My mentor helped me here. He told me to prepare for every possible objection they could throw at me because once you've given a half-decent response to an objection, the yearning to "knee jerk" falls away.

So, we wrote down responses to all the objections I could think of that would be thrown at me during those warm customer calls.

In your world, you will be acutely aware of the ones you get all the time. Whether you advise/sell mortgages, personal loans, life assurance or investments. When you make calls to your database of clients from the past, they will throw back concerns to you.

Typical Customer Concerns

Let's take the personal loan or second charge/loan marketplace, which is heavily consumer-oriented and digitised to the point where customers come to you via the internet. You need to give regulated advice to help them achieve their goals. You give the advice, send them the documents, and hear nothing. You phone them, and they say:

- "We don't need you anymore, but you were most helpful."

- "You were very knowledgeable, but we don't need you anymore, thank you."

- "You were great, thanks, but we're all sorted; thanks for your time."

- "I need to think about it."

- "Your fee is too high."

- "I've no idea who the lender you've recommended is."

- "I spoke with (competitor) and might be working with them."

- "I've found a much lower percentage loan online."

- "I'm going to use my existing provider."

And so on. Of course, there are a myriad more, but they boil down to 4 categories:

1.   They don't trust you.

2.   They don't think your solution will work.

3.   They think it's too expensive or they can't afford it.

4.   They don't have the time to deal with it, or no is not the best time.

Now plenty of these can be dealt with during the earlier conversation with the customer. Trust is built, a proper solution determined affordability and checking budgets and a quick inspection to see they have time to deal with it now. But people are people and will throw all sorts of knee jerk reactions at you.

Sitting On Their LAP

My mentor back in 1988 taught me the post-it note trick. We brainstormed answers to all the various objections that might be thrown around at me and wrote them down on a post-it note, and stuck it to my wall behind my desk. When a customer mentioned one of them, I swung my chair, read the answer, and returned the volley.

At first, I tanked.

Completely failed.

Bombed entirely.

Because I failed to listen to them, I hit them too hard and turned them away from me. My mentor told me I didn't sit on their lap. This mesmerised me. As a 24-year-old, the notion of sitting on my customer's lap was something that horrified me. But he suggested I do it.

LAP stands for:

- Listen

- Acknowledge their thinking

- Probe further to fully understand the nature of their issue.

It was the listening piece I missed out on; I'd failed to give them the common courtesy to listen and acknowledge what they were saying. I understand, Mr Khan; I see where you're coming from. Yes, I get you. I'm hearing what you are saying. But it was the probing that changed everything.

"Why do you say that? What exactly do you mean? What is it that you want to think over? I hope you don't mind me asking?" "What arrangement have they given you?" I appreciate where you're coming from; what deal have they come back with?"

Now I was listening, taking everything they were saying, understanding their point of view, building rapport, showing empathy. And it worked. My answers to their situation didn't put them on the back foot, so to speak; it was a real conversation and enough to dispel their knee jerk reaction.

LAPAC

So I mastered the LAPAC

- Listen

- Acknowledge

- Probe

- Answer

- Confirm and close

Over the next few months, I had a trickle of customers coming back into the office, chatting through their finances with me; I was helping with life assurance, building insurance. You'd be surprised how many of them hadn't any clue they could shop around for that.

One or two started chatting to the negotiators in the office to contemplate selling their house. It built an incredible connection with them, kept me busy and produced a small but increasing commission income stream for the office.

And saved my job.

The Definitive Protection Selling Dossier

Chapter Summary

Paul gives you his workshop Masterclass in writing. This chapter results from years of delivering a highly successful session to countless advisers and brokers, recording videos and podcasts on the topic.

Everything you ever needed to know to secure a high-value client protection business alongside your financing and mortgage advising. All wrapped up in a neat package.

The Changing Buyer

Customers have changed. We know that. Some will blame the Pandemic, but the metamorphosis has been going on for ages. No one wants to be sold anything anymore; we're fully aware of that too.

Protection needs to be sold, always has and always will. It's not the sort of product people wake up on Saturday morning and say, "Hey, darling, let's go out and buy some life assurance, shall we?"

Just won't happen, so it needs selling. However, "selling" is a dirty word amongst mortgage advisers, so what's the replacement? Easy that one. It's called helping them buy or coaching the client to accept protection advice. That's how we do it now, the modern way, fit for purpose.

Let me share with you how.

Your Motivation to Sell Protection

A quick recap to prove why we should:

- The FCA says we should since clients have identified needs and want us to serve those needs. It's our job.

- It's ethical to do so.

- People die and get ill, so we should protect them.

- Professionalism says we should.

- You want to sleep at night.

- Your firm or principal advises that you should.

- Commission says yes, it'll help pay the bills; you don't need to charge a fee for protection advice.

- The future AI bots will do it, so why shouldn't we.

Dealing With Client Questions and Problems

By handling any concerns and questions, they might have earlier. Before they become questions or issues.

It was a scorching afternoon in the Vendee, France, at Les Dunes Camping Site. We'd just arrived after a long drive, and Sharon, our Rep, showed us to our caravan, which was home for a few weeks. This is always a scary moment as you are in their hands to choose the location.

Would we be next to the family from hell?

Would we be next to the bar or, worse still, the Karaoke?

No, we were being led back towards the entrance to the park, with the main road and amusements. The rep turned around and said confidently before I even thought of the noise issue.

"The people before you were a little worried about being close to the entrance, but when they left yesterday, they told me what a great location they had. They mentioned how close the van was to all the amenities and how quiet it was at night."

I hadn't even thought about the noise problem until she mentioned it. Still, because she'd given me a customer testimonial and some benefits of the location, it didn't even cross my mind that it would be difficult.

Clever.

I wonder if she was a trained salesperson. But the point was she did just the right thing. Let me explain further.

No product or service is perfect. There are always downsides or disadvantages, or the competition has the edge in one or two areas. No one has a "killer application" for long these days as competition is so swift and reactive.

There's always going to be something the customer might not fully appreciate and just might lead to an objection later on, usually when we ask for the order or close the sale.

Now I'm not saying that you should tell the customer all the main problems of your product early on in the process. If there is a particular feature that the competition beat you on. Previous customers have mentioned it before, then pre-empt it.

Just like Sharon did with the caravan location.

It might not be a problem with your product or service. It could just be a hurdle your customer has to cross before enjoying the product. Something that potentially might cause them to stall when it comes to purchasing.

How do we figure out what's on the client's mind before vocalising their questions and issues? Difficult, we do have to engage with them to find out more. This is essential, but most clients will have questions around the four global concerns. Money, time, trust and the solution won't work.

Handling the Cost Issue

With the money, we get affordability problems. Protection costs a slice of your monthly income, a regular direct debit for years. It's a big commitment, and people may baulk at paying £75 per month. They are pretty happy to set up a Direct Debit with Sky TV or buy pet insurance for Fido at £40 per month, without blinking an eyelid.

With the cost, it's an excellent idea to allow the client to start thinking about this earlier. Mentioning the concept of protection during your introduction with the client will coach them to see where it all fits. Further coaching may reveal a budget for the mortgage and the associated protection. It may not.

So a further discussion around surplus income and whether they might consider earmarking some of their regular payment towards protection will pay dividends later. Possibly you'll want to coach them as to the cost at an earlier stage "we might be looking at £75 to £100 per month; how do you feel about that?"

When we talk about monthly premiums later, they won't be so surprised.

The other benefit of discussing the cost earlier is coaching the client to appreciate that a mortgage commitment comes with protection. It's like bread and butter or gin and tonic. They go together, and the monthly commitment should include all aspects of the mortgage and protection. Again helping them to appreciate this early in the process is critical.

Managing the "Not Now" Issue

The second area of concern for clients is time. Lack of it may be, but typically it's not the right time to talk about protection. You see, most are up to their neck in buying the house and all that goes with that stress.

The secret is to bring the discussion in early and get used to the idea. Build the chat into your sales process early, perhaps even take care of some of the underwritings to save time. If you're chatting about income protection, you don't need the mortgage to complete; people have the need immediately, so make the medical submission early.

Dealing with the "Won't Work" Matter

The "Won't Work" issue is because clients don't appreciate why they need protection. When you present some options, cover and premiums, they'll push back since they don't think they need to be paying an extra £75 per month.

To deal with this problem, you will want to bring into your factfind some coaching around establishing the need for protection. A healthy conversation around the impact on them and their family of the death, illness and suffering from a significant disease has to occur. More on this later.

As you can see, there are several concerns that customers will have around protection. With a carefully structured approach to factfinding and presenting options, you'll find yourself answering their concerns way before they come into their head.

That's how to give advice and promote protection. It has to be sold, but not forcibly; you need to iron out any wrinkles as you factfind your way to the recommendation.

Protection Success Blueprint

Let's look at your sales process and how you can fit in the discussions around protection.

I use three steps here:

1. Sow the seed
2. Coach the gap
3. Present the options

1. Sow the Seed

As the name suggests, this is your opportunity to bring to the client's attention the idea that you will advise protection alongside the mortgage. The best advisers say this very early on.

One adviser today that I was working with suggested he mentioned it during his qualifying call with the customer.

Usually, he runs a 20 or so minute call after disclosure to ascertain how much the customer can afford, the monthly payments, etc. He then confirms this with a decision in principle, which helps fend off estate agents and other house sellers who want to see proof before an offer is accepted.

During this conversation, he asks about the customer's income and outgoings. He talks about their expected budget to pay the mortgage and associated costs. This is a great way to help the customer afford the loan and grow accustomed to meeting regular commitments.

At this stage, he talks about protecting your mortgage in the event of death, illness etc. and chats about the monthly cost. This flexible budget figure becomes essential when actual costings are calculated and presented.

Another adviser I was coaching liked to introduce himself as a Mortgage and Protection Adviser during the initial disclosure part of his meeting. Literally, in the first 5 minutes, he would start talking about protecting the mortgage. Words such as "put together a full-service package, to allow you to buy your home and ensure it's fully protected in the event of death and illness" were used for sowing the seed.

2. Coach the Gap

This is a contemporary way of viewing mortgage advice. Younger and young at heart borrowers don't like to be told what to do anymore. Of course, they'll carry out copious amounts of research before seeing you. Still, when they're with you, they'd figure it out themselves.

You can do this by adopting a coaching approach to advice rather than the more traditional "this is my advice, take it or leave it".

Coaching ensures you ask lots of questions to help the customer and guide them along the process.

So rather than telling them that they ought to have life assurance, change your style. Ask them a question to find out what they know about life assurance and the impact of not having enough on them and their family. In the old days, we used to call these disturbing questions. I think that tag has lost its place today; it's rather scary.

As a coach, we're asking the customer various questions to see how a gap in protection will affect their family. What it means to their mortgage and their loved ones if a tragedy strikes. More on this later.

Advisers I work with vary enormously in how they coach the gap. Some don't and prefer to just tell the customer what would happen and get their commitment to looking at some options. Others really dive into the subject with carefully crafted questions. They also have immense empathy with the customer, ask softened questions and summarise and discuss things really well.

The coaches leave their customers worrying about the lack of protection with the promise that they'll plug this gap with some options shortly.

Finally.

3. Present the Options

Good advisers now can put everything into a full-service package of costs. A package includes the mortgage elements plus protection plans to plug the gap, including home insurance. Talking about a whole package allows it to fit the budget or possibly tweak upwards.

It can get a little cumbersome when the adviser must hand the protection sale off to another adviser. Larger broker firms do this when people tend to specialise. There's no right or wrong way in my experience. Personally, I think an adviser who controls the whole process and can source protection options themselves has more oversight with the advice and can ensure it gets put to bed, so to speak.

Sometimes handling off the protection to another team causes a disjoint and can occasionally mean the plans never get bought or the customer heads to google their dilemma. Pre-empting the problem or handling it yourself as the mortgage is secured is the best bet. But not always possible.

Sweet Spot Protection Selling

Advising and selling protection plans to clients does involve a fair bit of persuasion and influencing to ensure your client gets the coverage they need. And one day may thank for arranging it.

We've talked about budgeting, sowing the seed earlier and packaging.

This is not always possible. We'd be naïve to think it was. One of my coaching adviser clients works in the new homes marketplace. She has numerous meetings per day, several qualifying Zooms and plenty of calls. Her builder introducers just want the agreement in principle confirmed so they can shift the new home. She is left with little time or motivation to introduce protection early. So she comes back to it later; when the rush is over, the client has calmed down and has more time to spend on the topic.

She then factfinds the protection need helping the client realise their need and seek a solution. But no budget has been discussed. She operates sweet spot pricing cleverly.

Once the "need" has been established and quantified, my adviser knows precisely what cover is necessary, the sum assured amount, etc. She then creates three options for her client. Skiing downhill, so to speak, she starts with the platinum option. A complete suite of products to suit all the client's protection needs with cover set at maximum desired levels. Naturally, this is the highest cost.

Then she presents the gold level. Solid cover, generous sums assured, some features stripped out to conserve cost and presented as an affordable solution.

Then comes silver. Budget cover at a budget cost but still some protection to ensure the mortgage is protected on death and some income paid on illness.

The client invariably chooses the middle option because they didn't have a budget in mind beforehand.

Ultimately, we must ensure our client is protected adequately, but affordability does come into the equation. If it's too expensive, they will struggle to pay and have direct debit shock later. This will cause them to cancel and upset all sorts of KPIs monitoring the adviser's performance. That's the real world; welcome to it.

Mind the Gap

One of my favourite automated phrases from the London Underground. "Mind the Gap", they exclaim to warn passengers of the gap between the train and the platform in case they fall through and hurt themselves. In the same way, customers have to be aware that it can be disastrous if they fall through the protection gap.

We've been banging the drum around coaching as the modern method for mortgage advice adoption. Continuing this theme, we ought to coach the gap rather than just tell the client the impact of having this protection disparity.

You see, that's a significant danger here. Merely telling the customer that they have a gap is not enough. Some advisers back up this "telling" with a glossy brochure or two from the insurance firms. These show how many people will die or become seriously ill and the devastating outcome.

We used to use a video called "The Widow's Story" back in the day, which was harrowing. It visually depicted a couple and a tragic death like a horror movie. It brought us to tears.

Some advisers tell stories. I like this. I used to use a story, a real one, mind you. I arranged joint life assurance for a couple, and the husband died dreadfully one night at work. Naturally, I used to embellish the narrative, which got the desired reaction. The client was shocked.

However, the coaching must come through. Simply ask the client (I shall call them the client now, as you're doing business together). Ask them a question or two to determine what effect these disasters would have on their family. Death, illness, accident. How would it affect them, what would it cause, how would they pay the mortgage, etc.

You know the answers, you understand how death can impact a young family, you've learnt that in your exams and training. But you really don't want to just tell them. People have to see it themselves in their language. Appreciate the impact and devastation caused.

That's coaching. It's mighty.

Suggested Coaching Questions

Once they see the problems, you've coached the gap. You must then talk about how to plug the gap and the benefit this brings. Money to pay off the mortgage, cash to pay the bills. In trust, so it gets to you quickly.

Here are some photos of questions suggested by attendees on our live courses, which I captured on Whiteboard. If you can decipher my writing, there might be some good ones for you to use. Have them with my and my attendee's compliments.

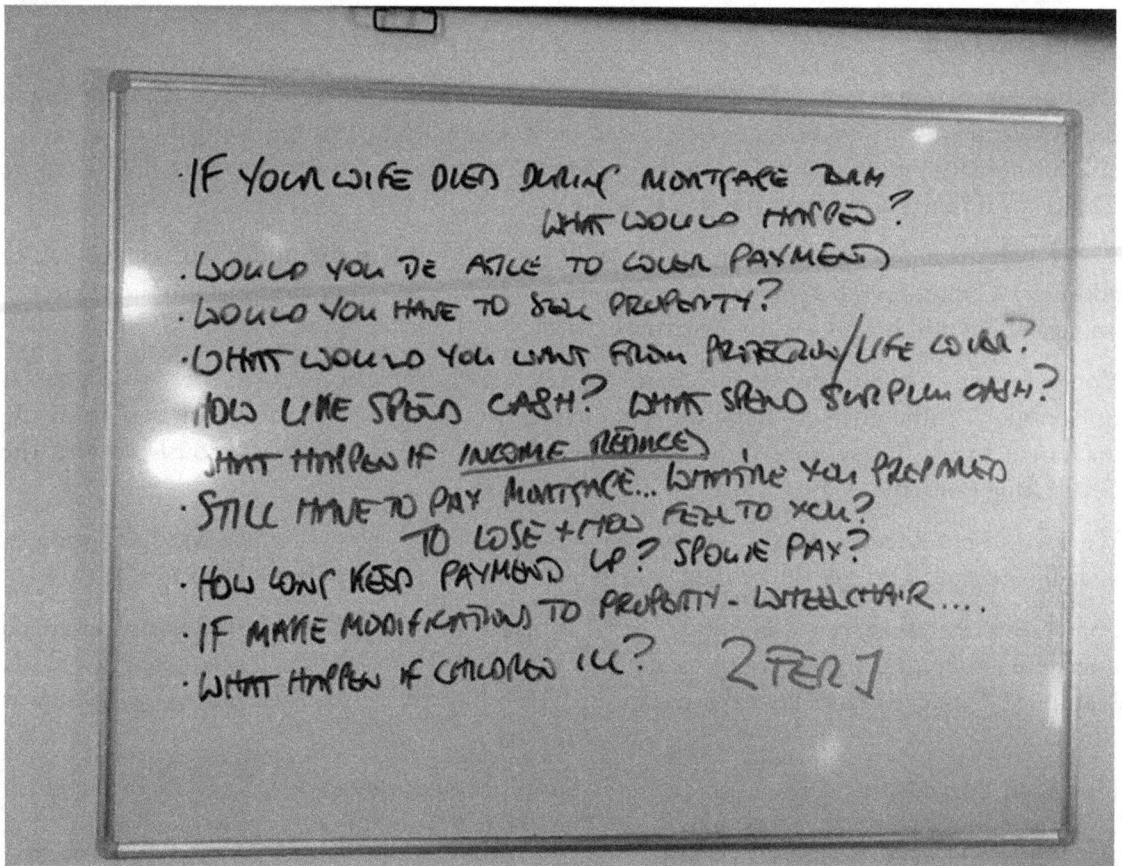

IF ONE PASSED AWAY - WOULD YOU WORK DURING
                    THAT PERIOD?

T WOULD YOU HAVE TO WORK
E LOOK AFTER CHILDREN/ PAX NURSERY / CHILDCARE
D WHAT HAPPENS IF LOSE BREADWINNING INCOME?
   HOW AFFECT YOU?
   WOULD YOU HAVE TO SELL HOUSE? MOVE IN OTH FAMILY?

· IF OFF WORK ACCIDENT/ILLNESS - STILL RECEIVE INCOME
· DO YOU KNOW EMPLOYER' PAYMENT OFF WORK?
· HOW WOULD YOU FUND TIME OFF WORK?
· WHAT'S BACKUP PLAN
· WHAT PLAN IN PLACE IF SUFFERING SERIOUS ILLNESS
· WHAT EXTRA COST INVOLVED IN ADAPTING HOUSE
· WHAT PROBLEM'S ARISE IF SUFFER CI   EDUCATE
· DO YOU KNOW ANYONE IN FAMILY   ACCIDT ON C/I
· WHAT WOULD CHANGE? WHAT GIVE U/ EFFECT ON FAMILY
                    HOW FEEL?

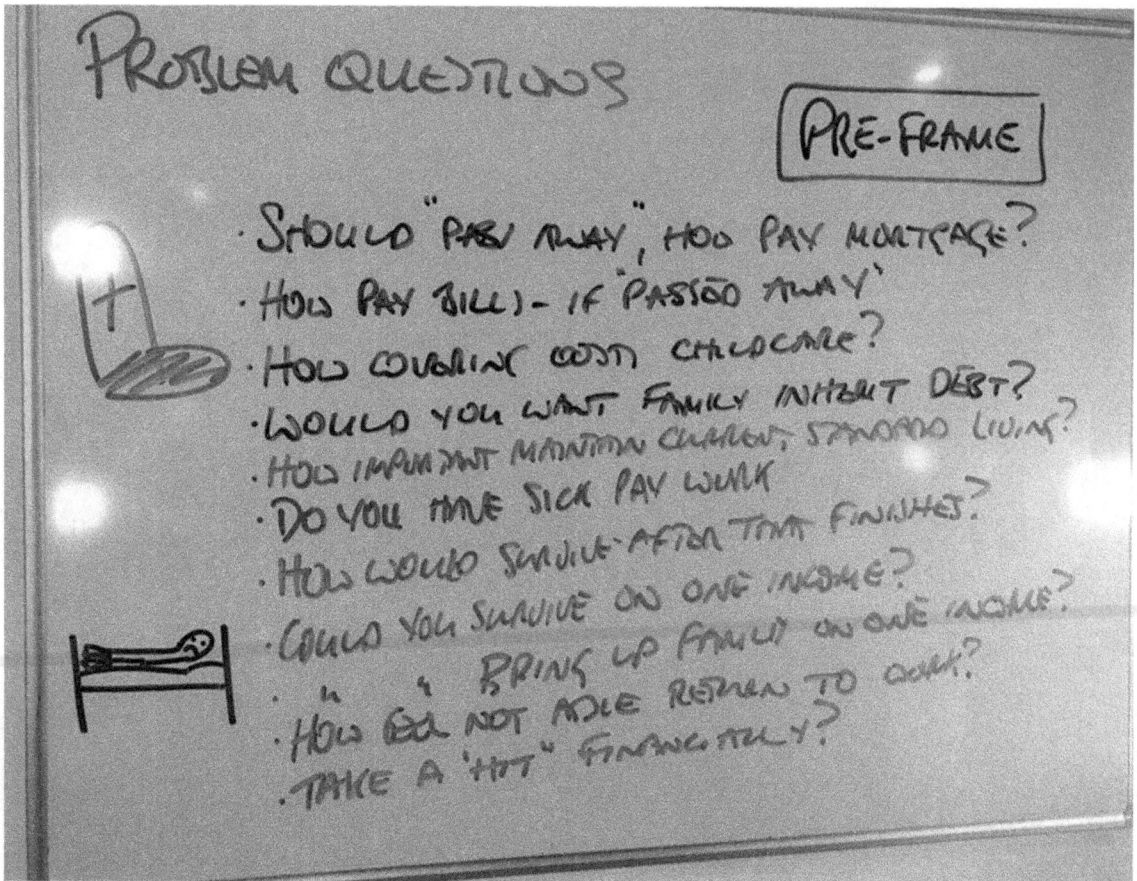

PROBLEM QUESTIONS PRE-FRAME

- SHOULD "PASS AWAY", HOO PAY MORTGAGE?
- HOW PAY BILLS - IF PASSED AWAY
- HOW COVERING COST CHILDCARE?
- WOULD YOU WANT FAMILY INHERIT DEBT?
- HOW IMPORTANT MAINTAIN CURRENT STANDARD LIVING?
- DO YOU HAVE SICK PAY WORK
- HOW WOULD SURVIVE AFTER THAT FINISHES?
- COULD YOU SURVIVE ON ONE INCOME?
-   "   " BRING UP FAMILY ON ONE INCOME?
- HOW IF NOT ABLE RETURN TO WORK?
- TAKE A 'HIT' FINANCIALLY?

How to Coach - Summarised

We call it CIGAR:

- C – Current situation. Factfind the client's existing cover, family situation, benefits from work and such.

- I – Ideal situation. What should they have in place to protect in the event of death, illness, accident?

- G – Gap fill. Coach the gap with questions.

- A – Action – take the proper steps to plug the gap. A set of plans that provide money in the event of death, illness and so on.

- R – Review. Annually look at the client's cover in place, review the sums assured, terms etc.

CIGAR is a handy reminder of the steps involved in the factfind.

Sugar Coating Your Questions

It was 1985; I was just 21. I was working for a small building society in Walton on Thames. I was the Assistant Manager and expected to do the selling in the branch. Selling was still a dirty word in the mutual building society game. Still, the company sent me on a week-long residential sales training course. It was located somewhere in Oxford in a unique training centre; I called it a mansion.

I learnt loads.

After the course had finished on Friday evening, I'd arranged a date. Her name was Caron; she worked as a receptionist at the Holiday Inn hotel in Shepperton. She was charming, and I really wanted to make a good impression on our first date.

The course finished at lunchtime on Friday, so I drove home in my Alpha Romeo Giulietta, a lovely set of wheels housing a 1.6-litre boxer engine; it sounded great.

On my way home, I thought about my date with Caron and how I could impress her. Suddenly an idea came to mind. We learnt that the secret to selling and getting the customer interested was to ask questions on the course. Find out about them, their needs, criteria and match your product to their needs.

Simple. That's what I'll do tonight.

The restaurant was a French Bistro in Thames Ditton. I had a rack of lamb; it was sublime. Halfway through the main course, Caron stood up, pushed her chair in and said:

"Paul, you're a nice guy, but I actually don't like you."

I was speechless, stunned, resembling a frog with his mouth wide open.

"As I said, you're a nice guy; I don't like you because you ask too many questions. I feel like I'm being interrogated."

They didn't teach me how to sugar coat questions at the training course, ensuring more conversation than an interrogation. I learnt afterwards that to sugar coat, you use your tone of voice, and you pre-frame them with permission tags such as "May I ask" or "Tell me" or "It would be interesting to know". You use plenty of verbal nods such as "Uh hur, I see, tell me more" rather than another question, and you maintain eye contact all the time.

That way, it "sugar coats" the questions.

Too late for me. I paid the bill, the total amount, by the way, fetched Caron's coat, drove her home in silence, walked her to her parent's front door and left with my tail between my legs. I never saw her ever again. And she was stunningly beautiful too. But I was only 21.

Gaining Commitment

Throughout the factfinding process, we're helping the client see the need for protection. We're using great coaching questions. When we "sowed the seed" earlier, we made it known that we'll be putting together a package of products to help the client buy the house and have it fully protected.

We discussed budgets and a figure that would be appropriate to meet the cost of this package. So the client is entirely expecting this.

However, it's courtesy to help them appreciate this as we talk about the "gap". The client is a little shaken up with your questions if you think about it. I mean, talking about dying or becoming seriously ill is often disturbing for the best of us. You owe it to them to reassure them that you're going to deal with this dilemma and arrange some cover within their budget.

All you need to do is tell them what you are going to do, and that's a good thing. Just get their head nodding that they like the idea. I call this the Vicar Close.

For those of you lucky enough to be married, you might have noticed the vicar (or the State Registrar) asking the congregation if anyone has any reason that you shouldn't be matched. In the same manner, we ask the same question to our clients. Rather than "is there any reason why you wouldn't buy the protection" you could ask:

"I'll be getting a package of protection put together that'll take all these concerns away from the two of you. I'll present this later; if it meets your needs and fits your budget, can I take it you'll be happy to go ahead?"

Neat.

Especially if there's going to be a slight gap between now and showing them the options. Maybe someone else in your team will be doing this, or you'll do it when they find a property. Dangerous since every day that goes by means they will forget your conversation.

It's best to show the options nearer to the factfind as possible, whilst it's fresh.

The longer it goes on, the danger of:

- Going online to research quotes
- Speaking to friends
- Chatting to other advisers

These might occur. You need to ensure they don't. So asking the client or doing a vicar close might be an excellent first step.

Here's a bonus for you:

6 Top Performer Protection Tips

Taken from some outstanding mortgage and protection advisers I worked with in August 2021. In no particular order:

1. Sweet spot pricing. If you haven't arranged a budget, then use sweet spot pricing. Present three sets of options. The Platinum, gold and silver. Aim for the gold to appeal most for affordability and cover.

2. During the DIP – Decision in Principle meeting, obtain a budget to afford the whole package. Although affordability is discussed here, you must ensure the client thinks protection and mortgage are within the same budget.

3. Quickly explain Critical Illness first before factfinding it. Clients don't understand it initially. "Do you know what CI is? Let me explain it first" Then coach the gap in critical illness.

4. Ask if they know anyone close who has suffered from a critical illness and survived. Everyone knows someone who has had cancer or a heart attack. Then coach the gap.

5. When discussing budgets or costs, help them compare the price to insurance that helps, not hinders. Keep away from pet insurance or phone insurance. Instead, focus their attention on car insurance and ask what the cost of that is. You're more likely to get £45 per month in return.

6. Be passionate about what you do as a protection adviser. "My job is to ensure….", "I'm really passionate about protecting my clients". Show this enthusiasm when you sow the seed; it's what makes you unique and absorbing.

How To Set Up a Virtual Video Studio

Chapter Summary

It's all-pervasive nowadays, and each winter brings semi lockdowns at a rapid pace; the requirement won't go away. Working from home makes virtual training even more desirable and essential each year.

But we know that, don't we?

This chapter has a straightforward aim. To encourage you to move beyond the laptop model to some kind of Studio or room where you can emulate real-world training and presenting. Even if everything you need is stored in a pilot case allowing for portability.

Or you adopt a permanent home for your studio; that's your choice. So long as you take the first step to untethering yourself from a "sitting at your laptop on the desk" scenario.

Let me explain how.

My First Foray into a Studio

My first foray into online presenting came in 2006 with a programme called DimDim. Don't get me started on that name; it's now long "gone-gone". Dimdim was acquired by Salesforce.com for $31 million in 2011. And it worked just fine.

Goto was available but terribly expensive. Both only allowed voice-over PowerPoint presentations with little or no speaker video, let alone attendees.

I realised it wasn't right even then. I dreamt of having the tech emulate or copy how we operate in a face-to-face environment one day. I kept this dream alive during the latter years and into the pandemic, knowing that this was the way forward. I wanted to emulate the face to face experience in a virtual classroom environment.

Along came Zoom, Teams et al., each capable of beaming full video of everyone involved. I could now copy real-world training rooms with rapid broadband speeds.

However, people still defaulted to laptops playing PowerPoint slides with a presenter narrating these from a small thumbnail image in the top corner. Most attendees blank their videos and mute their sound, and the whole experience was less than inspiring.

This may resonate with you. Not because you have many choices. Armed with the firm's laptop, a built-in webcam, and a dining room table, there's not much you can do to advance yourself.

The Studio is the Answer

In 2015, I began to build my first Studio, which may sound rather glamorous as it really was only a spare bedroom. In 2019 I began excavating a basement in our house and created an all-singing video studio. It measures 13 x 10 feet, smaller than most bedrooms, but it's big enough.

The Studio is the answer. Flexibility is also the solution. You may need portability, so I will show you how to fit the kit into a pilot case and wheel it around. However, a permanent structure or room housing your equipment is ideal.

You might consider a room at home, a spare room in the office or even convert an existing small meeting room into a video studio.

The Studio Emulates Real Life

Remember your aim is to emulate the real-life experience of a physical meeting room. Let's remind ourselves how this works. A trainer or speaker usually hovers around the front of the room, and attendees typically sit around a desk or a U shaped table.

At the front are the visual aids. A screen to project PowerPoint, a flipchart or a whiteboard. Some have Smart Boards, but these are just glorified touch-screen computer monitors.

The speaker can interact with the people, and she can use whatever visual stimulates and adds to the message. Everything is being used together seamlessly. She typically stands when presenting and actively engages the group in conversation around the topic.

This is your aim but to repeat online. Let me explain the kit you need to add to your purpose-built or converted room. Your space doesn't have to be significant. I operate from a 13 x 10-foot room.

Imagine a computer mouse on a mouse mat able to control a much bigger monitor, often 3 or 4 times its size. That's how it's done online.

Let's talk kit now. Which, of course, will evolve over time. However, many video kits, such as camera technology, matured a few years ago. After all, a Carl Zeiss lens is a Zeiss lens.

The Studio on a Minimum Budget

- Space to present – I have 2 metres square to physically move around in. Recall my mouse and mouse mat analogy. You're the mouse, and the space is your mouse mat.

- 2 computer screens positioned at eye level – bear in mind you'll be mainly standing or perched on a high stool. These are to see your people.

- Headset microphone – USB connected to give you the freedom to talk and hear your attendees – note no cable.

- A decent webcam on a tripod perched behind and above your monitors. See if you can buy one with autofocus and software to operate the zoom.

- A mouse clicker that moves your slides forwards and backwards.

- A whiteboard or flipchart plus pens (large ones).

- Lighting in front of you. Possibly on the ceiling or on tripods or stands.

- Broadband connected to your PC via an ethernet cable – don't rely on Wi-Fi.

The Studio on a Maximum Budget

- Blackmagic Atem Mini – video streamer.

- HDMI Cameras – DSLR – these are the ones with the lens that protrudes from the camera giving you the ability to zoom manually. Ideally, a couple of cameras provide you with a couple of fixed angles.

- Tripods to house the cameras and cables to connect the Atem Mini.

- 4 computer screens are attached to a well-powered PC (not a laptop).

- PowerPoint from a separate laptop connected to your Atem Mini gives you the ability to switch the view to your slides just by pressing one button on the Atem.

- A sound speaker system attached to your PC to hear your people.

- Lapel microphone wirelessly attached to your PC or Atem Mini.

- Whiteboard and/or flipchart – Whiteboards are preferred. Flipchart paper just doesn't look right on camera. Think of a Vienetta. Google this – they're delicious.

- A pull-down green screen allows you to appear in front of your slides in full view.

- A variety of lights on stands to light up you, the green screen and whiteboard.

The Studio as a Portable option

Shelley and I spend a lot of time in Edinburgh visiting our daughter Jess in their flat. We hire a small flat on Airbnb, which has fast Wi-Fi, and I like to run live online sessions whilst we're there.

So I have a mobile version of my Studio – not ideal, but it allows me to perform as well as possible. Particularly useful for small group events, one to one coaching and such. Here's what's in my bag:

- Laptop – obviously and hooked up to the Wi-Fi – the router is close by with no thick walls or microwave ovens in the way.

- Tripod and flat stand for the laptop, which will be at eye level.

- Ring light to perch behind the computer – this light attaches to a USB port on the laptop, so no extra power cable is needed.

- Logitech Brio Webcam with a clamp so that it hangs on the top of the laptop.

- Headset and microphone attached – USB connection to laptop.

- Extra USB gadget to allow more open ports on the laptop.

- Sticky whiteboard plastic. These look like cling film and come out of a dispenser. Take a slice and stick it to the wall. Hey, presto – one whiteboard.

- Software – I use Logitech Capture – to allow me to stream a picture in a picture for my slides and me. That way, the slides appear alongside my video image.

- Capture allows me to resize my video image perfectly and have slides to my right or left. Clever and simple.

- This all fits neatly into a pilot case, so I'm incredibly portable.

The Studio Photos

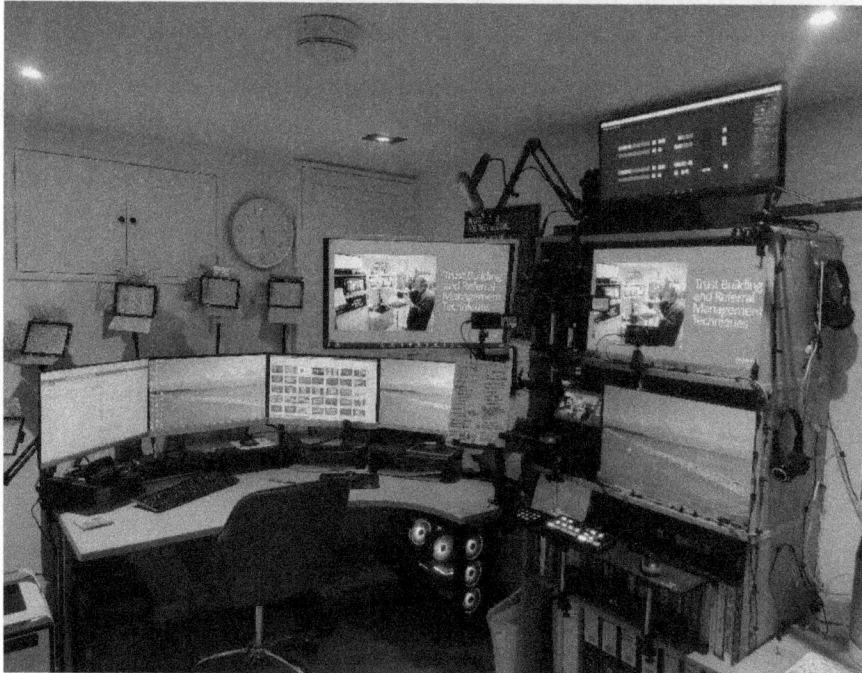

A Field Guide to Live Video Selling

Chapter Summary

This field guide was designed for you – the professional B2B or B2C salesperson – to quickly adapt to the Live Video Selling world. Inside the handbook, you'll see all of the processes, skills and techniques you need to master to achieve in this new medium, which isn't going away.

An essential Field Guide.

At the back of the guide, you'll find a convenient checklist that you can use to self-assess your progress. All Sales Managers will find this essential when observing your salespeople, which is straightforward when selling on video.

We'll be adding to the guide as technology evolves and improves rapidly over the next few years.

Adapting Your Sales Process for Live Video Selling

- Gone are the days, or at least post–lockdown, when in-person sales meetings happen, so maximise and accelerate your sales process to enable Live Video Selling.

- Shorten the meetings, and cut down the aims for each session—separate sessions for rapport and trust-building, discovery, presentations, negotiations etc.

- Meetings no longer than 20 minutes and scheduled off the hour, i.e. 10.10 or 15:25. This encourages attendance and punctuality rather than on the hour. Twenty-minute slots are more likely to be agreed or fitted around your customers' busy schedules.

- Tightly agenda every meeting.

- Schedule each meeting using Calendar Invites with Zoom/Teams invite logins and include the list.

- Bring in other team members into discussions to add variety and engagement – agenda their input strictly.

- Stretch your sales process if need be; decisions are made slower in a "down" economy.

- End each meeting with a call to action, summarise these via email using the same calendar invite entry on Office 365 and link these, Velcro fashion, to the next meeting. Always have a link for every meeting – a glue.

Creating Your Professional In-Home Studio – a Reminder

- A professional home studio doesn't always involve a dedicated room or study. However, this is preferable to ensure privacy and minimal noise and disruption from family/home life.

- At home, create a "Zoom Zone" or "Teams Terrain" where the background is conducive to a professional image. This zone, which sits behind you, should be pleasant to the eye and maximise the rule of thirds. Visualise your screen space with three vertical and three horizontal lines creating nine equal-sized boxes. Position your head and shoulder in the left or centre box with your eyes in the top bar. Place eye-pleasing items such as plants and photo frames on the other side of your space.

- The wall can be blank; it better to be so rather than gregarious wallpaper. Head over to YouTube to watch some professionally produced videos, and you'll notice this tip in action. Have your Team Terrain or Zoom Zone available to you in your home office or anywhere in the house that works. Remove any sign of a bookshelf – that's just been abused during the lockdown.

- I have a video studio for my online workshops with whiteboards and green screens, but you don't need to go to that extent.

- Line up your background before any video call, so it's perfect as soon as the call starts; there's nothing worse than adjusting your webcam as you're introducing yourself. It should be instantaneous.

- Be wary of digital backgrounds – they never look right and appear surreptitious. Have you ever bought from a website with no contact details, address or phone/email? Digital backgrounds seem to hide something. They never look good unless you have a well-lit Green Screen behind you. Be careful of the pop-up company adverts behind you as well. If you were in a client meeting in person, you wouldn't remove a pop-up banner from your briefcase and display it behind you, would you? So why do it on Live Video Selling?

- Dress well and appropriately for your meeting; you can slightly dumb down your appearance. The ties are usually only for professors appearing on the nightly news.

- Eliminate noise wherever possible. A closed-door does the job. Use Zoom's AI setup to remove unwanted noise – it's remarkably proficient at doing this.

- Rid yourself of any distractions. Cats and dogs were OK during the lockdown, quite the novelty, but that newness has now worn off.

- Too far away? Or too close. Can you fit your head and shoulders onto the screen without being too distant or in "their face?"

- Be aware of the angle of your webcam. Place the camera lens so that it's level with your eyes. Place this on some books or a purpose-built stand if you're using a laptop. If you have a moving webcam, purchase a gooseneck tripod and position the camera so that it's level with your eyes.

- Focus on your office set up in your conference room or work desk. These tips can be imitated in your in-person office, particularly any open-plan office you use. Backgrounds can be tricky, but an office scene is harmonious so long as it's neat. Sound is the big issue, and a stylish headset is a must for in-office Live Video Selling.

- If you have a conference room setup, then you probably also have a budget to kit it out professionally to enable groups of you to present and receive customers on video. Logitech does some perfect kit, so google them.

Prospecting, Lead Generation and Discovery and Presenting Tips

- Social selling can be adopted seamlessly with Live Video Selling. The use of the internet to find, research and discover potential customers and prospects is essential. Arguably, this is marketing, but modern professional salespeople adopt Personal Marketing concepts and do much of this themselves. Marketing teams are migrating into different focus areas now; professional salespeople conduct personal marketing.

- Old fashioned cold phone calling is a relic of the 1990s – some still advocate this but look at them closely, and they probably still live in the 90s or at least gained their sales spurs in that decade.

- The key is connecting seamlessly marketing with selling. Selling starts with a rapport and discovery stage with Live Video Selling doing the work.

- From the LinkedIn typed chat, encourage a meet, the first face to face contact. Do this via Video for 10 minutes, assessing joint chemistry and rapport. Phone calls can work, of course, but many of your potential customers, in the B2B space are readily available via Video Call and prefer this method. Suggest, and you will be rewarded.

- Use screen-share regularly to provide variety and visual stimulus – websites, PDFs, sales aids, video – can all be shared well.

- Collaborate with your customer if you feel it would add value. Use a shared PowerPoint or whiteboard and encourage the customer to co-operate online. For example, you could put the five main challenges other customers face and ask them to annotate with a "tick" or "cross" next to the words. Or you could use icons or pictures to add flavour. Naturally, you'll want to ensure the customer is "up for this" – some are, some aren't – and the kit they're using may or may not be conducive; for example, a touch screen may enable them to draw quickly. Collaboration builds commitment.

- Stand and deliver, sang Adam Ant in 1980. The girls loved him; your audience might adore you more if you stood and gave your presentation. Have a delivery zone where you can move around a little, autofocus your camera and put it at eye level, avoiding nostril view. Try it and see

- Use "you" more than the omnipresent slides. Many speakers like to hide behind the slide deck, relax in their chairs and talk. These webinars don't cut much nowadays; your audience wants more of you. So more you, fewer slides.

Sharpen the Saw – Skills to Develop

You want to sharpen your skills with your new kit and sales process.

- Mature your empathy capability. Understand their position and point of view. Are they at home, suffocating with lockdown, panicking over the down economy or struggling with too much business?

- Become adept at reading faces. Body language reading is for in-person meetings – the stroll from reception, the small talk in the elevator, and the chat over coffee – all allow you to assess their body language. On video, that's not possible. Focus on micro expressions, facial colour tone, learn eye movements (NLP up, down etc. – thinking styles).

- Be aware of your resting face. Do you grimace, smile, glare or look downright angry? Your customer will be looking at your face continuously and making judgements just so you learn to create a halfway house resting face. Not the put on smile that most Zoomer's put on when they see their face on the screen, but a cross between thinking and a smile.

- Listen loudly and pause more regularly. Pausing helps the other person jump in the say something, particularly useful when more than two of you are on the call. When in-person, it's the subtle cues that help us step in and talk. You don't have this on video, so pause more and allow the conversation to be two-way.

- Summarise more often when live video selling. Summaries are valuable sales tools anyway, primarily important on video as they allow the customer to digest everything, confirm you've heard them and move the conversation on. You'll be running shorter meetings on-screen so summaries can stop waffling and diversifying the conversation off track.

- Your ability to ask quality questions is even more vital when live video selling. You might get away with second-rate questioning in person because your body language and non-verbal skills encourage the customer to say more. On video, this can't be relied upon. Use open questions, of course, but learn to use Power Open Questions. These questions cause the customer to respond, "that's a good question." Think back to the last time a customer said this to you, and you probably just asked the finest question of your sales career.

- Power questions are short, open, curious, genuine and valuable. "Talk me through…" is an excellent example, "what brings you to that thought?" is another.

- Use stories to illustrate. Live video selling can be tricky to concentrate on, especially when presenting with few visual aids. Turn this into a short, engaging story, and you'll regain the customer's attention. Craft your stories – google story selling for ideas – learn and curate them for varying needs. For example, have stories ready for – comparing with competition, your crucial selling points, previous customer objections, client success stories, why they should use you rather than Acme etc.

- Refine your facilitation skills for when you bring others onto the call. For example, you may bring in the product specialist, legal people or your sales manager to help with the call's objectives. Become the orchestra's conductor; otherwise, they'll dominate or won't know when to contribute. You take control and bring people in and out of the conversation. Live video selling requires conducting.

- Ramp up your vocals and sound. Either get some software to do this or learn to sound like a TV presenter or newscaster. Smarten up your vocal cosmetics – pace, tone of voice, resonance, range, emphasis.

- Eye contact. Since lockdown, the internet has well documented this skill; however, staring at your camera lens is not the answer. No one ever won a sales contract by staring at the customer's eyes throughout the hour-long in-person meeting. It's not natural, so neither is continuously staring at the camera lens. Newscasters do this because they speak to a camera with millions of people watching. You're not. You're engaging with an individual, so adopt your in-person eye contact routine with the lens as a part of their face.

- Position your camera lens as close as you can to their eyes on the screen. You can use a gooseneck tripod to place the webcam right in front of the screen – you can give them proper eye contact and look at the lens simultaneously. Alternatively, move your gaze from their eyes on the screen to the camera lens naturally, so a few seconds on their eyes, then over to the lens for a couple of seconds, then away to the left for a second or two, back to their eyes and so on. Make it natural.

- Test closing. Without body language to read, the imaginary traffic light signal of red, amber and green is impossible. This buying signal technique works very well in person but not on-screen, so adopt verbal test closing more. "How does that sound, Jenny?" or "what are your thoughts so far?" or "Are we both on the right lines here?". You could sprinkle in a yes tag if you want, couldn't you. How's this article reading for you so far?" It's proving rather useful, isn't it" "You'd like to finish it, wouldn't you?"

- Note-taking is an art whether you're in person or on camera. Note-taking on camera can appear stilted and disingenuous towards the customer, so learn to jot down key points or mindmap. Suggest to the customer that you want to make a few notes and say when you are. More signposting of your actions is needed on camera.

Trust Building on Camera

- Trust building or maintaining a rapport can be a little trickier on camera. In-person gives you many more opportunities – talking about the game on Sunday works well, or chatting about their family outing whilst riding the elevator. Or matching and mirroring their body language and style.

- On camera, adopt a few additional measures. Use social media to collate a picture of your customer. LinkedIn can help. Googling can reveal aspects of the person.

Using Visual Aids – PowerPoint

- Using visuals is essential; PowerPoint is the go-to. Live video selling with PowerPoint requires dramatically different slides.

- Follow the 3 to 4-second rule with visuals. Every 3 to 4 seconds, there needs to be a change: an animation movement, a new slide, something different. A one-word slide followed by another to mirror your sentence works well—large imagery. Think Hollywood movies and Steven Spielberg – always exciting, continually moving. Keeps attention.

- No bullets please, we're British. Or American. Bullets are a relic of the 1990s and kill people.

- There are many more tips available to maximise your PowerPoint; invest in some online training; you'll be glad you did.

- Collaborative whiteboards replace the paper we all used to use. A real whiteboard can be helpful behind you but requires special lighting and positioning. Virtual whiteboards can be used easily with a touch screen or stylus.

- Blend your face with your visuals. Many of your customers will be using a monitor with just enough space for your visuals. Use software to blend your face and your visuals. Zoom and Teams now can do just this. Don't hide behind your visual aids and be just the voice behind the scenes. Live video selling is not running a webinar; they were invented in the 90s and should be banished to that decade along with Grunge music, Blockbuster Video and Tamagotchis.

Video Selling Checklist

Professional in-house studio adopted

☐ "Zoom Zone" or "Teams Scape" created

☐ Background synchronised before the call

☐ Digital background fit for purpose, green screen

☐ Noise eliminated

☐ Distractions minimised

☐ Webcam level with eyes

☐ Camera image using the rule of thirds

☐ Good lighting in front and above

☐ Visuals used "real" whiteboard, flipchart, hand-held board

Tech Check

☐ Internet via ethernet or Wi-Fi stable

☐ External webcam used

☐ HD image on internal cam

☐ USB mic used

☐ Headset used

☐ Large or multiple screens evident

☐ Tech Plan B is available

Competent with using Tech

- ☐ Setting up meetings
- ☐ Document sharing, programmes open with handouts etc.
- ☐ PowerPoint Screen show
- ☐ Annotation on screen for collaboration
- ☐ Pinning video
- ☐ Cloud or local recording
- ☐ Sharing video clip with sound
- ☐ Screenshots – hard copying
- ☐ Muting sound
- ☐ Gallery/speaker view toggle
- ☐ Competent use of all controls in Zoom/Teams

Online Sales Skills Checklist

- ☐ Empathy evidenced
- ☐ Trust built
- ☐ Matching customers where appropriate
- ☐ Facial language read and used
- ☐ Resting face conducive
- ☐ Signposting agenda throughout
- ☐ Listened loudly
- ☐ Paused more often
- ☐ Summarised often
- ☐ Power questions asked
- ☐ Stories/metaphors used
- ☐ Facilitation skills evidenced
- ☐ 80:20 Rule in Discovery
- ☐ Voice pace matched with customer
- ☐ The vocal range of voice used

- ☐ Voice volume appropriate
- ☐ Eye gaze maintained
- ☐ Visual aids used
- ☐ Test closing used
- ☐ Note-taking without distracting
- ☐ Stand when presenting
- ☐ No hiding behind slides

PowerPoint Competence

- ☐ Shared effortlessly
- ☐ Switching between full camera and slides
- ☐ 3 to 4-second movement rule
- ☐ Visual stimulus
- ☐ SmartArt used
- ☐ Bullets list more graphical
- ☐ Collaborative digital whiteboarding
- ☐ Face and visuals on the same screen

How To Present Visually Virtually

Chapter Summary

A step-by-step guide to using visuals online to enhance your virtual presentation rather than a dull, listless voice-over PowerPoint.

I've been a keen student of online presenting since my first webinar in 2006. Being constrained to sharing PowerPoint with a voice-over seemed old-fashioned to me even in 2006. I yearned to emulate real-life presenting but in the online space. But the technology wasn't available.

It is now, but very few presenters use it preferring to display a shared screen of PowerPoint visuals with a voice-over coming from a tiny face in the corner.

It can be different. And it should be. Let me show you how I've become quite adept at it. Presenting like in real life but online.

The Real-World Comparison

Let me take you back to the last in-person presentation that you enjoyed. I think you can recall a good presenter engaging with you, giving you eye contact and expressing their character. Attractive, with stories, metaphors and clear diction. Maybe some humour but particularly stimulating.

She has visuals, probably a large screen showing excellent PowerPoint. She stands to the side, maybe in front, as she moves around the "stage". She interacts with her visuals which add massive value to the topic. She is the main focus of your attention and uses visuals to back up and further enhance the message.

Not always expected in the corporate world, but I'm sure you can remember a similar real-life presentation.

The trick is to emulate this in the online environment. Let me show you how.

Why Do We Need Visuals Online?

The whole point of online presentations is to utilise the power of visuals; otherwise, you might as well just be using the phone. And there's inherently nothing wrong with the phone.

Using the online platform allows coaches and trainers to add pictorials to help the person understand what they are saying. Salespeople can use visuals with clients to describe complicated concepts. Sales managers can use them to help with their coaching and 1:1s.

The main reason for using visuals is that the world is geared that way now. We all have large TV screens on the wall, view adverts on bus stops and train stations that move. Carry phones with magnificent visual displays and are glued to the internet on our laptops and tablets, with a plethora of images.

Younger generations probably are more visual now than any generation before them, having been weaned on tablets and phones since a tender age.

Visuals are ubiquitous.

Who's the Primary Visual?

The presenter, that's who. Most platforms default to the presenter sharing a screen on PowerPoint and remaining virtually hidden whilst she narrates the slides and presents the topic.

Since this is the default for most presenters, it has become the "go-to" way of presenting. I believe this is nonsense. Presenters need to learn to present to the camera lens as though they were standing in a boardroom talking to a group of people. They should "stand and deliver". No sitting at your desk talking to a laptop.

Standing is natural when presenting; you have energy, poise and volume. Find some space in your office or room where you can talk from. Your stage, so to speak.

It's not an ample space needed – 2 metres by 2 metres is more than enough to move a little, gesture with your arms and enhance your message through body language.

Position your camera at eye level to you. A tripod, a gooseneck attachment will allow you to position a separate webcam. Or you can perch your laptop on a highchair and a few books if you have to.

On the topic of webcams, ensure you have a model that is good with autofocusing, as you will be moving backwards and forwards as you speak.

Have some lighting ahead of you, behind or above your camera. You could even light the wall or background behind you. Although this isn't essential, just light your front.

Care with what's behind you just as you would when presenting for real. Because your audience will look at whatever is there.

Finally, your microphone. The superior option is to don a lapel microphone that connects wirelessly to your computer. This gives you freedom of movement. An alternative is to have a boom microphone just under the camera. The worst option is to use the webcam mic.

Now you're dominating proceedings and controlling the presentation like a conductor in the orchestra, you can point to visuals to help you support and enhance the message.

The Default Shared Screen Option

Zoom, Teams and all platforms give you the option of sharing a computer screen or application, so your audience gets to see this on their PC screen. Tiny thumbnail mages of you and the audience appear along the boundary. Still, most of the monitor is taken up with the shared screen.

All the platforms attempt to help your video image appear more graciously alongside the shared screen. These can be clunky and difficult to control whilst in full presentation flow.

You can share anything that's on your computer. PowerPoint tends to be the bookie's favourite as we all use it when presenting in real life. PDFs, a web browser, and even a digital whiteboard can be displayed.

There are hundreds of apps you can fire up offering all sorts of visual stimuli. Zoom and Teams both give you instant access to these apps. But essentially, you're just sharing a screen with your audience, and sitting tends to be your default position as you have to operate these apps from your computer. This is why most presenters sit when presenting online. Close to their mouse.

Shame that.

Let's remember that when you present in real life, you don't have the option to operate a computer mouse. On a good day, you had a clicker in your right hand, small enough to be hidden as you gestured with your audience. We'll keep the clicker online, which you use to advance PowerPoint.

Simultaneous Streaming of You and Your Visuals

Now we're stepping things up a little. Imagine the old school presentation. Your audience would see you alongside the slides. You would orchestrate the whole scene, bringing up visuals when needed. You can emulate this online with a video streaming app.

Let me explain.

Rather than relying on your webcam to send a video stream to your webinar platform, you choose a stream created by the software. This way, you select a different video option created by the software.

The software allows you to combine your PowerPoint visuals alongside your video image. Some call this picture in picture.

There are dozens of software options to choose from, and I suggest you try a few out. Capture, Vmix, Prezi; the list goes on.

I use a Blackmagic Atem Mini Extreme to do all of this for me. This clever box of tricks controls what goes into my video stream. I have eight options. My PowerPoint visuals and four camera angles in my studio. Three spares at the moment of writing.

Imagine a BBC News studio with three or four cameras showing the newsreader from different positions. I can also combine these four options to allow picture in picture. It's pretty cool, and the ultimate coolness is the four large buttons on the console that you just press once to change the view everyone sees. No fiddling with a mouse operation whilst in full presenting flow.

The picture in picture operation shows me presenting and, alongside me, my slides. I can position my sliders next to me, above me. In fact, anywhere on my screen. However, the best feature is the green screen or chroma key feature.

Behind me, attached to the wall, is a green screen that I can pull down from the ceiling. This lets me display my visuals behind me. Weatherperson style. I can interact, point to images and words and move from left to right.

Just like I used to do with an authentic audience presenting in front, I can concentrate on my presentation and my audience behind the camera lens with the touch of four simple buttons.

Livestreaming v Zoom

The last point in this section might push you beyond the boundaries of Zoom and Teams. Once you can produce a video stream created by your software, you can livestream rather than present via Zoom. Live streaming is very different to Zoom. It's a dedicated app that streams your video anywhere, live. You can stream to YouTube, a website, Facebook. The list goes on. Livestreaming allows real HD quality from your end, and your audience can pick it up on any device. Exciting.

Other Visual Options

Remember the old school presentations? Many speakers and trainers would use a flipchart or whiteboard. There's no reason why you can't do this either. So long as you have good lighting in your room, you can position a flipchart or whiteboard to allow you to use these in front of the camera lens.

It's that easy.

My Atem Mini has a camera angle to present my whiteboard behind me. I use big whiteboard markers to allow my audience to read my drawings. I like the whiteboard. It's different, very interactive and will enable me to build a picture or story as I speak.

Just like I used to do in real-world training rooms.

Mixing it Up for the Ultimate Effect

Every successful real-life training or speaking event involved mixing it up. Never would a presenter simply sit there and talk to a group for hours on end. She would present for 5 minutes, then shows some visuals, maybe some flipchart work. She might then sit down and run a group discussion interspersed with group activities.

Presenters may run a short Q&A and facilitate brief group activities but primarily present. And that's where visuals come into their own. They allow the message to hit home, help the audience engage and enjoy the topic and ultimately take action.

Remember, it's about emulating what you did in the actual boardroom. It can be done, is being done to significant effect, and you are now expected to up your game and do the same. Gone are the days when you can "get away with a slide deck" hidden discretely behind the slides sitting at your desk with a ropey webcam and tinny sound.

You owe it to your audience.

CPD'ing for Mortgage Advisers

What Does CPD and Pathe News Have in Common?

Firstly get your CPD recording automated. You can download apps to record these or buy a small learning diary to document your learning.

CPD is either structured or unstructured - structured is formal learning such as online courses, workshops. Unstructured is general reading, podcasts and videos that keep you up to date.

You need to choose your mediums for unstructured and plan to consume them every week/month without fail. Determine your learning style - VARK works here. Visual, auditory, read-write or kino. I'm read-write and audio. So I:

- Read voraciously. My Kindle is full of books; I read one a month on average. My current books are The Sales Coach's Playbook: Breaking the Performance Code - Bill Bartlett.

- Consume regular magazines offline and online. I read Money Week, The Week and The Economist every week. These are paid-for subscriptions. Monthly I receive Mortgage Strategy, Money Marketing and Building Society Gazette (these are free)

- I subscribe to various newsletters and blogs. My favourites are Seth Godin, Mortgage Introducer, FTAdviser, Mortgage Solutions, The Economist Expresso, Allan Weiss and Graham Jones; I don't subscribe or read BBC news anymore. I researched this, and the BBC news is now 80% opinion of its journalists. I don't want to hear Laura's exasperated tone anymore or constant criticism of the government. If you're going to see how news should be broadcasted, google "Pathe Newsreels". This was before the 1990s when news went 24 hours, and they ran out of the stuff, so they replaced it with opinions and expert reviews.

- I belong to a couple of associations to keep me up to date. They run online meetings and workshops—the Professional Speaking Association, Sales Performance Association, Personal Finance Society.

- Podcasts are a brilliant way of learning and multi-tasking. I listen to mine in the gym. I subscribe to Spotify because that's easy on my phone. I listen to various sales, advising and general updates on Podcasts. There are thousands, so be brutal with those you will religiously consume. Advanced Selling, Advisers Assemble, Meaningful Money, Sales Gravy, Allan Weiss, Voices of Experience

Remember to invest time each week. I do 3:1:1 - 1 day a week self-development on average. You sell what's in your brain; you don't make widgets, so make sure you keep it sharp.

Ten Traits of a Self-Directed Learner

What do Bill Gates, Mark Zuckerberg, and I have in common?

We're all self-directed learners. I've proudly been a self-directed learner since 1994, when I realised that no employer of mine was ever going to provide me with the training and development that I needed to make a success of my fledgeling career. Twenty-five years' of self-directed learning, and I feel I've succeeded in evolving myself for the future and have done so through self-employment where I didn't officially have a training budget.

It's worked for me and will work for all future learners in the workplace; gone are the days when students gorged on company training programmes. The future is for those that make it happen.

Here are ten traits that you need to master to become a self-directed learner in no particular order.

1. Initiative

The first trait is initiative. Suppose your learner has set themselves a goal to learn something. In that case, they have the ambition and capability to find suitable learning. They are adept at searching the internet for reading materials, audio and video and can also venture offline. They just seem to find what they're looking for. Care your "Great Fire-Wall of China" doesn't block anything of use – most corporate IT departments block helpful sites. They don't trust people.

2. Independence

Independence comes next. With their learning goals in tow, self-directed learners don't need permission to learn; they feel empowered to do so. Some companies even provide a budget to further their independence. My employed position in 1997 awarded me with a training budget of £1,000 a year and I was trusted and empowered to use this to buy training. I used it to part-fund my early NLP training.

3. Network

They network well. Possibly members of various associations and unions that provide relevant learning and development. Networking with fellow members and others offers ample learning opportunities, sometimes over a coffee or fireside chat. Learning doesn't have to be formal. My best ideas and insights have come from random conversations with people in my network. My special education events have come from my membership of three associations – PSA, SPA and AAISP. Google them.

4. Responsibility

They embrace responsibility for their learning. The buck stops with them; no one else will help them develop; it's something they're accountable for.

5. Plan Own Development

Self-directed learners plan their own development time. I devote a day a week to personal development, not every week, but on average. Only with this amount of time investment can I achieve my learning goals.

6. Curious

They're curious to learn things. A goal can lead anywhere. In 2012, I committed to master how to create a video for my business, and boy was this a giant learning curve for me. Ten years later, I'm producing some half decent videos. Still, my curiosity took me to other areas beyond just video production.

I'm currently using live streaming, so my video work streams live to YouTube, Facebook, LinkedIn and Vimeo. My inquisitiveness also took me into Research and Development grants and tax advantages, which saved me a packet over the years.

7. Learning as You Go

Self-learners don't mind starting something at 80% ready. Too many people start projects or activities when they believe they are 100% prepared to go. Self-learners believe in learning as you go, and this often requires that you create something and learn/improve as you progress.

That's the modern way. I watch some of my early incarnations of videos still on YouTube. I am pretty awful compared to my current videos. But at the time, they were new, exciting and achieved my objectives.

8. Aware of Learning Style

Self-directed learners are good at erudition and can adopt basic study skills. I'm aware of my learning style acutely. I know that reading works for me; listening to podcasts gives me the freedom to learn where I want. I know I have to make notes when I learn. I use mindmaps (a technique I learnt way back in the nineties by reading books).

I work well in conferences and listen to an outstanding speaker for hours. Incidentally, I don't do learning activities in groups – that's not my cup of tea. I'm very aware of how I learn.

9. Unlearning

Self-directed learners understand the unlearning process. When you learn something new, you have to unlearn the old first. Otherwise, you're just piling on new on top of ageing, and you will struggle to see new ideas and innovations. Before you decide to learn something new, you unlearn the old.

For example, when learning about trainer video, I had to unlearn all the presentation skills I learned when performing in front of a group – interaction, questioning, eye contact, movement, gestures – do these things when being videoed it'll all go wrong. You look at the lens on the video, keep your gestures minimal, preferably nil, and maximise your facial expressions and voice.

10. They Enjoy Learning

Finally, I enjoy my learning. It can be hard work, tiring and prone to errors and mistakes, but this gives me the benefits I seek. There's always a point, a scary moment when you don't understand what it is you're learning. This can cause stress, and you feel vulnerable. You have to drive yourself through this because you will realise it with a tenacious attitude.

With your people committed to self-directing and controlling their learning, the next step is to re-organise your learning and development offering to fit this learner. That'll come later once you've influenced the culture of your workforce first.

Measuring Your Adviser Development – KPIs for Learning

You measure everything else – results, profits, numbers, leads, sales and so on. We really ought to measure our learning.

Learning comes in two segments:

1. Learning you do yourself – reading, podcasts, YouTube, attending online classes, webinars. This is the lower-cost option
2. Learning facilitated by your manager or coach. This is expensive.

Measuring the first one is straightforward but challenging to gauge effectiveness. We can count the numbers, i.e. the number of books read per month, magazines and blogs consumed in a month, courses attended. People try to test the efficacy, but that's as useful as a chocolate teapot.

How many of you have done a multi-choice test at the end of eLearning and learnt diddly squat?

That's all well and good since you're investing your own time and keeping up to date with your learning. If it doesn't work or give much value, you've just wasted your time and a bit of money.

A regulated adviser will be supervised, monitored, and coached by their business or network, so here's how you can measure your advisory skills KPIs.

Adviser Skills KPIs

- Training time needs to be measured and logged. Many advisers have a minimum number of hours CPD they need to maintain their status – 50 hours, 36 hours, 15 hours – they're all different. Choose a number and work towards it. Easy to measure, but it only shows quantity, not quality.

- On quantity, see if you can let your recording systems log "training" time in addition to advising time, break times etc. That way, the adviser values the time spent learning a tad more. This also allows you to measure CPD, which comes next.

- Setting and monitoring your CPD goals can be a measure. Do you establish them each year or each month? Do the monthly goals feed on the annual goals and so on? For example, one of my CPD goals this year is to master a new gadget that plugs into my PCs and controls complex functions with one click. Say you want to switch cameras on Zoom? Usually, this process is cumbersome, especially in front of a live audience. The process occurs without losing eye contact with the group online with one button press. But the Elgato device needs learning, so I set a goal to do so.

- The number of coaching sessions is easily monitored. One hour or half-hour online sessions can be kept logged and possibly targeted. Say, once a week for a new adviser, two a week for a pre-competent adviser. One a month for an experienced adviser.

- Skills score. A coach can observe all skill processes. For example, factfinding with a customer, obtaining a referral, selling the need for protection can all be observed. Draw up a skills observation aid. Anyone suitably skilled can monitor and assess whether the steps are carried out and what degree of expertise. This can create a skills score. Put a target on this, such as 80%, observe the process and score them. Not too tricky but very subjective unless you tighten up the assessment criteria.

- Time to achieve this benchmark is another helpful measure. This shows how good the coaching is, how receptive the adviser is, and how competent they are. Again, this can have a target; particularly useful if you're scaling your advisor team and bringing as many people to the benchmark standard as quickly as possible.

- Finally, technical capability can be assessed and given a score. Naturally, a multi-choice test works and is not problematic to administer. Better still, do quarterly "tests" in the form of presentations at the online sales meeting, case studies to produce a readable suitability letter, role-plays of technical demonstrations, overcoming objection role-plays.

What gets measured, gets done, goes the narrative. Suppose your adviser or coach measures the success in this way. In that case, you can easily upscale your team and automate this extremely subjective area and bring value to your investment.

The Four Chemicals of Sales Motivation

Chapter Summary

Paul outlines the four chemicals produced naturally by the brain to stimulate and motivate people into action. EDSO – endorphins, dopamine, serotonin and oxytocin. More importantly, Paul shows you how to engender these to boost your motivation.

The Four Chemicals of Sales Motivation

One of my favourite cocktails is a Vodka Martini. It has four different ingredients – vodka, vermouth, olives and ice – it's delicious.

In the same way, it's been discovered and popularised by Simon Sinek that happiness or motivation is created in the human brain with four different chemicals. They're known as EDSO – endorphins, dopamine, serotonin and oxytocin.

They explain why humans are motivated and why salespeople do what they do.

Endorphins

This afternoon, I played squash with my best buddy Paul; he beat me at 2:1, it was close, and I played better than I usually do. When the game started, my right arm ached a little. I thought this would hurt, but after 10 minutes of warming up, my brain created endorphins, which eradicated the pain, and I could continue.

Although I lost, it was close, and I felt euphoric afterwards. However, I can feel a slight ache now as I type on the keyboard.

Endorphins do precisely what they are designed to do. They mask pain when exerting or exercising and give you a high to reward you and encourage you to return.

You create your own endorphins by:

- Smelling some vanilla or lavender.

- Taking some exercise.

- Seeking out daily laughter.

- Eating some dark chocolate.

- Listening to music.

- Eating something spicy.

All sales leaders should provide opportunities for their team to generate endorphins. They can give exercise time and equipment, gym passes, showers at work: Engender fun at work, laughter as a culture: Allow music, have a playlist of tunes that motivate and change your state.

Dopamine

In my first sales job back in the 80s, I'd thrown my pen in the air and cheer when I closed a deal. Boy, it felt good. Little did I know that was dopamine kicking in. I loved it, and it inspired me to get more sales. It can get addictive, though, and occasionally, I could come crashing down when the deals dried up.

Accomplishments trigger dopamine. Goals, achievements and objectives are ticked off. To-do lists are favourites with many salespeople. The ritual of crossing off and finally completing the whole list gives them so much pleasure – a shot of dopamine.

Though dopamine's fundamental role is to encourage more achievements, however small these are, finding food was enough to trigger a chemical burst in ancient times. Finding food meant you would stay alive, and it still works by merely eating.

That's where dopamine can become dangerous since it's massively addictive, similar to alcohol dependence or gambling habits. Checking your phone every 5 minutes gives you a hit, particularly if you've received some likes on your Instagram posting or Facebook update. I see people in my gym, admittedly the younger generation, picking up their phones every 5 minutes. A vibration in their pocket means they must look; it's addictive, and it's dopamine causing the compulsion.

Sales leaders can help their sales team get hits of dopamine. They can reward them for achieving the small goals that lead to ultimate victory, rather than just the final triumph. They can show them how to break down big goals into bite-sized chunks, which can be attained quickly.

Serotonin

Serotonin kicks in when we feel good: Pride, status and being part of a winning team. Whenever we feel significant, it triggers the release of serotonin and sales leaders can provide lots of this for their salespeople:

- Positive feedback.

- Recognition of success from peers.

- Opportunities to grow with career direction.

- Self-development breaks.

These are all classic motivators we've known about forever. Here are a couple of new ones:

- Since the brain can't distinguish between real or imaginary successes, trick it by imagining future achievements. I call this mental rehearsal, and it's not just valuable for eliminating nerves about a future event. Still, it'll also generate some rather handy serotonin.

- Likewise, recalling past successes can give you a boost of serotonin.

- Enjoy a burst of sunshine – this will top you up with vitamin D, but also some serotonin.

Oxytocin

This is designed to foster human relationships which continue humanity. Oxytocin is generated when you feel connected to someone else or in love. Trust and intimacy, physical touch and embracing your friends or lovers inject you with lots of it.

It boosts the immune system and makes you feel safe. Generosity and helping others give you a shot too.

So, make sure you:

- Hold regular team bonding outings to create trust and attachment.

- Encourage mentor programmes so others can help your people and get some oxytocin to boot.

- Hold regular one to ones with your salespeople to stimulate caring and progress.

- Give your advisers a hug a day. I'll leave this one to your discretion.

Summary

So those are four chemicals that create happy, motivated and productive salespeople who can influence their leaders. At long last, we have the ingredients, and I can keep enjoying my Vodka Martini. Even James Bond wanted one too, but his was shaken, not stirred; I never did understand the difference.

Mortgage Adviser Limiting Beliefs and Performance

Chapter Summary

Paul explores the 3 central limiting beliefs that he's seen consistently over the last 35 years in the financial services sector and shows you how to rid yourself of these hostile philosophies.

The 3 limiting beliefs surround closing, money and your client base.

Read on to discover how to tame the tiger of underperformance.

What are Limiting Beliefs?

Don't panic; it's not an illness. They are all over us; we're ravaged by them and affect our performance as advisers. We all have them to some degree.

It's the way we are, what we hold dear and believe in. Values are given to us at a young age which we'll defend at all costs.

I can't do that, or I'll never say that, or it'll never work, or that's just not me.

In over 35 years in the financial advising world, I've noticed three distinct limiting beliefs: closing, money, and client types.

Closing

Or better put, helping the client to make a decision. The issue here is that none of us wants to be pushy or "salesey" in the fee-based world. That closing, or heaven forbid, overcoming client reservations can make us come over like an old fashioned life assurance salesperson that we may have been trained as in the 1980s or 1990s.

So our limiting belief is not to close or ask to go ahead or even make a decision. Instead, we let the client decide in their own time.

Now, this is not at all bad; after all, if they're paying a fee for your advice, whether they decide or not is entirely up to them. We've made the recommendation and our competent staff will be able to process their instructions when they're ready.

The issue is compounded if it's fund-based charging we're using, without a decision, then no charging occurs. If we want them to commit to ongoing advice charging, we must help them decide.

What's the negative consequence of the client not deciding or, worse still, putting off a decision until later? It might be disastrous; the timing may not be correct. Aside from that, we've taken time to arrive at a recommendation, do vast amounts of research, weigh up the facts and emotions, taking counsel from others in the team. Our recommendations come with substance, so why shouldn't the customer decide. Our advice is correct, we've made sure of it, and it's worth its weight in gold…so they ought to decide one way or another. Putting it off is not a satisfactory conclusion for a professional relationship.

It's intrinsically wrong not to decide.

Money

This one comes down to our perception of money and value. It has numerous implications, especially in the modern world of adviser charging. When all is said and done, it's down to how you value yourself and the advice you give. People are buying you; you're either comfortable with this or not.

Think back to your upbringing, your nurturing, how did you feel about money then?

It all began when I was 12 and my first paper round, which paid a princely weekly wage which I spent every penny. I never had much money before that. I had a loving upbringing, but we didn't have money swilling around the place in our post-war council house. I left college in 1982 amid a significant recession, record unemployment and whole industries being decimated. As a Training Manager for financial services firm in the 1990s, another recession bit hard. My expenses were routinely annihilated, so my hotels became the budget varieties.

As a result, I value money, hard work, and industry in return for a fair wage. I constantly have to secure my self-belief and confidence around capital when I offer my fee schedule to clients. It's a lot of money, in my humble opinion. I need to focus on the value this fee provides.

But other people regard it as a poultry sum of money and don't think twice about securing the fee.

The answer is to grow comfortable with money since others view it differently. One person's £1,000 is another person's £1,000,000. It's all about value, not cost.

Would you bend down to pick up a 10p piece on the High Street?

Here are four strategies to help you.

1. ROI. Return on Investment. For every cost, there's always a return. Make sure you are crystal clear as to the value you provide. Calculate and estimate the return or the value that the client will accrue from your advice.

2. Work out how much they might save or might not lose. Estimate the emotional value of the right advice, the peace of mind. Make sure you arrive at a figure that justifies the fee.

3. Make visible what's invisible. An enormous amount of work goes on behind the scenes in your role as well as mine. For you, it's the back office team, the years you spend learning the ropes and studying for your exams, your CPD and all the articles, papers, trade magazine that you consume each week. The infrastructure, platforms, processes, software, computer algorithms all ensure your client gets the right advice at the right time.

4. Ensure your client appreciates all of this and how it supports your performance and your fee.

5. Clients buy your uniform. Now I know you don't wear a uniform, so to speak. You play a professional position in an established and reputable firm.

6. So when you're talking money with your client in the form of a fee, think about the uniform they're paying for, not you personally.

3. Let a third party sell you. We are the worse at selling ourselves. I'm a modest person; this is a value my parents instilled in me, so selling myself appears bragging or, worse, boasting.

No one likes a boastful soul. So find a way for a third party to sell you and justify your fee, and the best third party is your other clients. The secret here is to master a client referral programme. All your new clients are referred to or introduced to you by their friends or associates. Their friend is recommending you and justify your fee.

The best introduction goes like this: "Give Paul a call, listen to his advice, do everything he tells you and pay him whatever he charges you" That's referral nirvana.

You're expensive, but you're worth it.

Dealing With Clients

What kind of people are you comfortable with? Are you relaxed with rich people, extraordinarily successful and fulfilled people, or do they scare you? A rhetorical question, but our client base that we choose to advise may well be more prosperous than you, substantially better-off than you with wealth possibly inherited through the generations.

You may not have much in common with affluent people or think you don't, so you may not feel you deserve to advise them. You may have been educated at a State School; they might have attended public school and a Red Brick University.

Now you'll cope with this in varying ways. You might be ok with it; you might not, but if you hesitate a tiny bit, this will affect how you present yourself with high-net-worth clients, and they'll sense it within 10 seconds.

Your limiting beliefs around who you should advise will affect your business levels significantly if your client base average wealth has increased over the years.

The trick, which I use myself, is to re-frame the situation. Re-framing is a particularly clever technique that literally changes how we see something. Your client is not dealing with you because you play at the same golf club. They are working with you in partnership because they trust you, have faith in you, know that you are an expert worth paying for and if you get along and have rapport, more the better.

You are not their friend – that was a 1980s technique we taught you – that doesn't cut in the RDR world. They are paying for a professional financial adviser who can understand them, listen to their needs and goals, partner with them and provide substantiated and practical advice for them to act upon.

Mental Resilience for Stressed Mortgage Advisers

Chapter Summary

Paul outlines the dangerous disease affecting all salespeople from time to time – stress – and gives you some straightforward ways to handle this and build mental resilience.

Being More Mentally Resilient

It's often said that success in any role, particularly sales is 95% psychology, and the remainder 5% is all in the head.

Moreover, many salespeople struggle with the head game, succumbing to setbacks that cause stress, pressure and anxiety ending up doubting themselves and their abilities.

Lots of pundits have the answer and will sell you, their solution. NLP has many tools, inner game solutions are touted, and hypnotists get in with resolutions.

Today, though, I will give you a simple yet elegant idea that can help you stand up after setbacks and pushback, all those negative occurrences that set off your inner demon. Alternatively, you're a salesperson. You can self-coach this technique very quickly. If you're a sales manager, help your people by coaching them.

It's not copyrighted or owned by anyone, and it's regularly used by the NHS and other professionals to combat stress and other mental anxieties, and it works. The NHS use it as a cheap alternative to drugs and have trained thousands of people in it.

Let me explain.

What Causes Stress

There's always a situation or person that causes stress. A deal drops out of the funnel, bad feedback, a series of losses, and you're below target. Your boss has put you under pressure, or worse still, you've put yourself under pressure.

A manageable level of stress or adrenaline is right for you. Still, stress can get too much – there's a fine line between healthy pressure and stress-inducing pressure, and everyone has their limits.

These highly stressful situations cause feelings inside you, determining your following action. It could be a feeling of hopelessness or uselessness. Maybe resignation or just plain panic.

Dealing with Stress

Many salespeople try and deal with these feelings with mixed results. Here's the better way. Link back to your thinking at the time. Capture what you said to yourself before the sense emerges.

It could be the feeling of despair followed by a series of missed sales and a month that's looking way off target. You might say to yourself, "this month has turned out to be a disaster, it won't get much better," or "every deal this month has turned sour, there's no point in carrying on" or "the next broker is bound to say no as well since that product is much more expensive than everyone else's."

It's these thoughts that we can change. If so, it'll have a domino effect on your feelings and your actions following.

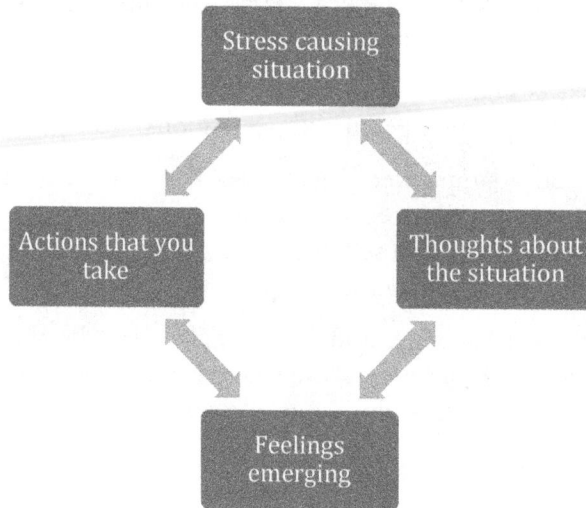

The Salesperson's Stress Handling Sequence

A stress-inducing situation occurs, you talk to yourself about it; this creates a feeling inside you that determines your following action. Change the thought process, and you can change your actions. It's called CBT or Cognitive Behavioural Therapy. I prefer to call it the Salesperson's Stress Sequence or SSS.

Use it when it's all getting too much in your head.

Here are the steps:

1. Step One – Capture the situation, thoughts and feelings

2.   Step Two – Recognise the thoughts

3.   Step Three – Challenge the thoughts

Find a space to reflect on the position and give yourself a little time to process it. Figure out your feelings as a result but carefully analyse your thinking that occurred immediately prior. This is important.

Categorise your initial thoughts to see if they are any of the usual's. We call these Knee Jerk thoughts. Here are the usual suspects to the reason behind your opinion. Most people tend to have two or three that dominate. See which ones resonate with you when you are caught with negative thinking.

Recognise Your Thoughts

All or nothing thinking

- You see things in extreme or in black and white.

- "It is either perfect, or it is a mess."

- "The broker likes me, or he doesn't."

Over-generalisation

- You see a single adverse event proof that other similar events will turn out the same.

Mental filter

- You pick out a single negative detail and dwell on it, viewing the whole situation as unfavourable.

Mind reading

- You conclude that someone reacts negatively to you, but you do not check this out with them.

Fortune telling

- You anticipate that things will turn out badly, and you feel that your prediction is already a fact.

Catastrophising

- You exaggerate the importance of things, such as something you may have thought was wrong.

- You inappropriately shrink your achievements or desirable qualities.

Should/must statements

- You set your self-standards of what you perceive you 'should' or 'must' be doing. These standards are often too high and unrealistic.

- The emotional consequence is guilt.

Labelling

- This is an extreme form of over generalising. Instead of describing your error, you attach a negative label to yourself: 'I'm a loser."

My "demons" are Should/Must Statements, All or Nothing Thinking and Mindreading. Remember, we are all human; never forget that everyone has these, even the author.

Challenge Your Thoughts

The aim here is to change the thought logically. Ask yourself these questions:

- "Am I making any thinking errors on this?"

- "What is the evidence for this thought and against it?"

- "What are the other ways of viewing this situation?"

- "What other supporting thoughts can I have?"

Be honest with your answers; no one can hear you or judge you on your replies. These questions allow you to rephrase your thought to something more positive. Say this new thought a few times, and it will domino your feelings.

It's helpful to capture this sequence in a table and keep some form of a journal:

Situation	Thought	Feeling	Challenge Thought	New Feeling

After a while, you'll be able to do this in your head without writing it down. This is a handy tool as a salesperson because every day, we have those little negative thoughts or demon thinking that can get us down unless we handle them.

Other Situations That SSS Can Assist

The urgent issue is stress-inducing thoughts that relate to a temporary underperformance situation. The SSS sequence can also handle these.

- Having to do an hour of cold calling

- Calling a marketing list

- Calling upon customers in the pipeline to close them

- Planning a large presentation

- Monthly one to one with your boss after a tricky month

- First meeting with a new client in their boardroom with four members of their senior executive team

- Conflict with a colleague

- Final stages of a challenging negotiation with a customer

Try it, it works, the NHS uses it and countless salespeople and their managers, and it's free and SSS no one knows you're doing it.

How To Keep Your Mortgage Clients

Chapter Summary

Paul explains how and why it's so important to keep in touch with clients and advise them for many years to come. Easy and straightforward, really, when you consider the logic of this, but you would be surprised how many brokers don't.

St Peter and the Gates of Heaven

St Peter is waiting at the Pearly Gates of Heaven as a newly recruited man approaches. "What would you prefer, Sir, Heaven or Hell?" "I'm not sure. Can you show me heaven please, and I'll decide". So St Peter shows the man around the most luxurious, safe and warm place. Full of birds singing, children playing and extreme happiness all around.

"I'll have that one please, heaven" So St Peter shows him through the gates, and the man arrives. Instead, he's confronted by a world consumed with fire, brimstone, lightning strikes. The smell of decaying everywhere, crying and screaming around every corner. He quickly pops back to the gate to confront St Peter.

"What's going on? You promised me luxury, safety, warmth and happiness. I saw the preview with my own eyes. What's going on?"

St Peter replied. "Sir, this morning you were a new client of mine, I needed to impress, but now you're an existing client."

An old story, you may have heard it before. Still, it nicely describes how many companies distinguish between new customers and old existing customers. All their attention and love is adorned on new customers, and existing ones are left to languish on the database with little care and attention.

I wonder how many mortgage brokers do this.

Tips to Keep in Touch

I'm sure it's not you, but in case it might be, allow me to share some principles and tactics you may wish to adopt as you set up and mature your mortgage advice practice:

- Unless you keep in touch with your existing clients, they will forget about you and infringe upon your competitors. They won't feel ashamed to use them for their next financing need.

- Regularly reviewing protection advice is essential, morally correct and profitable. Schedule 12-month reviews with all your protection clients. Set these in the diary in advance for both you and the clients when the last meeting ends.

- Don't ask them. Just let them assume that this is the way you operate in a professional capacity.

- Set up a CRM system – to house your client data and use it to keep in touch with your client on a semi-regular basis. Vary your communications. Emails with helpful information and updates maximise social media, ensuring you're connected on LinkedIn and Facebook via your business page. Birthday and Christmas cards never harm; you could even automate this via Moonpig. Find innovative ways of keeping in touch.

- Conduct the review meeting yourself or allow your new advisers to do this. Treat the review meeting as a chance to catch up and see if anything has changed.

- Organise the review meeting to be virtual. No need for your client to rock up at your offices or for you to drive miles and miles to their home. You already have rapport and trust, so a video meeting with all parties is just as powerful and far less demanding on people's calendars and busy lives. Clients are more likely to accept a 25-minute Zoom meeting than find 2 hours from their diary.

- You should consider charging for your reviews, they cost you time, and this fee puts a value on your time in the client's mind. You may charge a retainer so the client can retain your services. Other professionals do this, so should you.

- Some brokers I work with set a final stage in their sales process a good three or four weeks after completion. This 25-minute Zoom meeting ties up any loose ends and ensures the client can have their questions answered, etc. Some brokers use it to advise further protection, but it's also helpful to talk about referrals and the next steps.

- Fix rate anniversaries or other product maturities are essential times to get back in touch. Ensure you do so promptly before the lender has contacted them or the client has ventured online for a solution.

- Ensure you advise and sell general insurance such as house and contents. Brokers don't consistently market this product, but it is renewed every year and makes an ideal opportunity to get back in touch with the client.

Remember how expensive and time-consuming it was to secure a new customer. Existing customers come for free, but you need to expend time and effort to make that happen. After all, you'd like all your clients to be treated as new customers every time. Plus, be afforded the luxury of choice at the Pearly Gates.

Final Say – Top 10 of Everything

10 Rules for a Grounded and Solid Self Esteem

Crucial to all advisers. See what you think of these "rules":

1. Focus your energy on the present and future. The past has had its day – learn from mistakes and celebrate wins but don't dwell on the past.

2. Make peace with yourself; your views and attitudes are yours. Try not to worry about what other people think about you unless they are your better half. Mind your own business.

3. Your intentions should rule what you do and how you operate. If these are solid, ethical and right – you won't go far wrong.

4. Learn to compliment yourself and seek reassurance from inside of you. Don't rely on others to give you positive feedback – they generally don't.

5. Criticism is widespread nowadays, especially online when the giver is invisible. Smile graciously, but if you didn't seek it or agree with it or you don't respect the donor – ignore it.

6. Tragedy plus time equals humour. Every catastrophe or calamity in life can be loosened or watered-down with time. And when we look back, we often have a little chuckle. Some humour appears.

7. Care with judging others; there really is no mileage in assessing other people's deeds compared with yours. You'll always be superior in your mind. When you see someone and want to judge, just think about their story; that's usually enough to justify what they're doing. In their heads anyway.

8. Stop sweating the detail too much and be careful of overthinking things. Let serendipity figure things out for you or a shower or dog walk,

9. Limit your news intake. In the world of 24-hour news, even the BBC are sensationalising the news.

10. Exercise early in the morning before the day starts. That way you'll feel more energised.

10 Actions During an Economic Downturn for Mortgage Advisers

1. Only focus on the things you can influence and change, so forget about saving the world or changing society – think tactical. Five areas to focus your mind. Your loved ones, feeling healthy and protected, making enough money to pay the bills, preserving your base, i.e. your home and keeping your mind healthy and occupied.

2. The cashflow preservation society rules. Take a snapshot of your cash flow situation, where your money is going, your bills and outgoings over the next few months. If you run a small or medium-sized business – cash is king right now. Research what you can do to preserve some money. Government incentives, tax postponement, VAT postponement, furloughing. Cut out Sky Sports and unnecessary costs. Secure your income streams as far as you can.

3. Ring fence your clients and customers. Reach out to them to see how you can help in their current situation. Leave it at that. Most will be thankful; some will take you up on the offer; most will wonder how you can help, so be prepared to have an answer. Covert them, so they don't go anywhere else.

4. Do what you can to eliminate all risks they may feel when doing business with you with clients and customers. Risk is the most significant issue when heading into an economic downturn. Give strong guarantees.

5. Diversify more than you've ever done before. Focus on your core offering and think of ways to add value to your clients. Mortgage advisers should rethink their reason to be. You help clients in all aspects of property purchase and financing. You protect them in case things go wrong; you tidy up the legal and financial affairs of owning property, you maximise their borrowing capability. So think trusts, protection, life assurance, fire insurance, Power's of Attorney, Wills, debt management, refinancing, second charges, equity release, shared ownership. Diversify away from just proc fees.

6. Keep a close eye on how the mortgage world is coping and evolving. Things are changing. Soon, you won't see the same lenders on your sourcing system; other lenders will appear. New competition for your services will appear from nowhere in the next few months. Entrepreneurs are strangely active during an economic downturn. What was expensive in boom times becomes cheaper, so it's a good time to expand and move into new markets. If you don't, others sure will.

7. Rethink where you will operate from moving forward. Do you need an office, I mean really? Virtual is the new reality, and your customers will be moving on this too. Don't be a dinosaur.

8.   Accelerate your ability to prospect for business. It won't land on a plate anymore; you'll need to seek it. That means getting skilled at personal marketing. Pick up on Facebook advertising, lead purchase, referrals, partnerships, and so on. Tighten up your referral management and lead generation systems. Get serious with a CRM system at long last – these little gems can earn you plenty of business. They don't have to be costly. Nimble is $18 per month; Capsule is just £10 per month. Don't rely on memory; use technology to generate new leads.

9.   Think about your business model along with the competition for your services from humans and technology, i.e. AI. Is it a necessary purchase from clients, or can it drop down the list? Young first-time buyers might put house purchases further down their priority lost now that their careers need more attention. Can you pivot into becoming an IFA that specialises in the latter life marketplace? Very little competition there but a helluva lot of work is required on your part to get there. There are plenty of equity release advisers but very few qualified to help the latter life client with all their needs. That's worth paying for.

10.   Set goals, of course, but keep them flexible. Now is the time to have tactics – everyday actions that help you through these changing times, not long-winded strategies.

11.   And I didn't mention the word recession once. But we're already there technically and anecdotally. Plan and act differently; the world is and has changed.

10 Factfnding Tips to Keep you on the Ball

If you're in the business of factfinding or exploring the needs of your customer before you give them advice or a recommendation, here are 10 quick tips to use as an MOT or checkup:

1.   Focus on your non-verbals – your eye contact needs to be solid or appropriate for the customer, open body, gestures when talking. Use your head when listening – tilt your head to show interest, raise your eyebrows to signify curiosity.

2.   Freewheel first. Ignore your scripted questions on your factfind to start with. Just ask a solid open question around the topic you want to discuss and listen. Freewheel and see where the conversation goes.

3.   Remember your verbal "nods" to encourage the customer to carry on talking. "Uh hur", "I see", "interesting", "go on."

4.   Pre-frame your questions. Mainly if it's rather sensitive. "May I ask…", "Out of curiosity", "It would help me to know…."

5.   MAP-it out. When the customer answers an excellent question, and you think there's more, use the MAP discipline. Move away from thinking about your next question or the solution to what they are saying; clear your head. Appreciate them

entirely by focussing on just them. Playback to what they just told you and add areas you perceived or sensed. You can carry on MAP'ing customers for a long time, and it works too.

6.   Soften your questioning with your voice tone. Be aware of your voice tone when talking. When asking questions, your tone should lift slightly to indicate a question.

7.   WAIT – ask yourself – why am I talking – if you think you are doing this too much.

8.   Remove physical barriers. Tables, computer screens, books, noise.

9.   Ask short, open, curious questions one at a time; refrain from machine-gunning your customer with multiple questions strung together.

10.   Finally, some poetry. Kipling's Six Honest Serving Men. They taught him all he knew. Their names were what, why, when, how, where and who. Use these all the time.

10 Online Video Meeting Tips

I spend around 75% of my time online, on video, with clients either live or recorded. I've been conducting business this way ever since we came out of the financial crash in 2012 and fully expected this to continue unabated.

The percentage may increase as the world of Virtual Reality and Augmented Reality comes tumbling in.

So I've made all the mistakes you can imagine, but like you, I learn from my mistakes, so here are my ten tips for you.

1.   If it's a meetup with several people, treat it like a proper meeting. Make sure you have agendas, objectives etc., and you're mindful of the timings.

2.   Any materials you're using – PowerPoint decks, PDFs, etc., should be easily accessible online – upload them to the software to start with or have them open on another screen. Invest in some additional meeting space by having more than one monitor. I use four simultaneously; it allows you to have multiple documents at a glance.

3.   You'll be sharing screens, so make sure nothing can embarrass you or distract the group. Backgrounds, programme icons or shortcuts and worse still, any programme pop-ups. Disable them all and turn off any sound notifications. Treat your desktop just like a meeting room. Remove your landline (remove batteries) and mute your mobile. Disable the front doorbell and hush your dog.

4.   Use a headset with built-in mike; otherwise, you'll get that awful echoing and noise distortion. Leave that to early 90's shoegazing bands. If you don't have a headset, make sure your mike is far away from the speakers as possible. Better still, buy a Bluetooth headset – they cost £50.

5.   You need adequate lighting when appearing on video. Nothing fancy. I use a 9 LED light set up when recording a good video. Still, I use a three-light setup for live video meetings—two to the side of me shining on my face and one above the webcam.

6.   In a face to face meeting, you would give people eye contact, so do the same on video. It's tricky; I agree because their picture is not where your camera is. Purchase a flexible webcam holder that can position your camera just above or below where the images of your group are. That way, you can continuously look into the camera.

7.   Preview the video of yourself before the meeting so that your head and shoulders appear in the camera. Ideally, zoom to your head. Switch off the "follow face "function.

8.   Avoid fuzzy stripy clothes and be aware of what's behind you on camera. Naturally moving objects and people are a distraction. A window will kill your lighting, and a bookshelf is a bit old hat nowadays. It doesn't make you look more intelligent.

9.   Have backup WiFi in case of shut down, even if you have your phone ready to toggle a WiFi zone. After all, you will be setting up 15 minutes before the start time, won't you?

10.   And finally, you can wear what you like below your shirt or blouse but beware, you may have to stand up on the odd occasion, and your Hawaiian shorts may not be the right image to give.

10 Tips to Engage with Customers Over Zoom

1.   Have a chair with a firm back and keep your body relatively still, especially your head.

2.   Enlarge your camera so that your head and shoulders are seen. Customers will want to engage with your face, expressions, eye contact and mannerisms on video, not your arms and body.

3.   Raise your webcam so that the lens is level with your eyes. You don't want to look down on your customer, do you? Or give them a view of your nostrils.

4.   Summarise more often when on video, test the customer more too. Ask how things are landing, how they feel so far and so on. "Are you picking up what I'm putting down, man?"

5.   Share your call structure, schedule or journey. Take control and divide your meeting into a smaller session if you wish.

6.   Use their favourite video programme. If it's Facebook live, use this, or Teams or WhatsApp. Consumers will mostly be happy with Zoom, Facebook or WhatsApp. Business customers, probably Teams or Zoom.

7.   Care for your background; blank is suitable. Be extra wary about making comments on their locations; it's probably their home after all. Blurring out your background looks super cool, but false backgrounds look shady, especially if you don't have a green screen behind you. And most of us don't. Accelerate to a dashing Zoom Zone.

8.   Gaze at the eggshell shape surrounding their eyes, forehead and lens of your camera. Read their facial expressions, watch them closely but don't stare.

9.   Practice your listening skills and prevent yourself from interrupting. It would be best if you never did this anyway, whether on video or real. More time is needed in-between conversations on video. It's the extra half-second that makes all the difference,

10.   Pareto's 80:20 works just fine. They talk 80% you talk 20%. Keep to this ratio, and you'll not go far wrong.

10 Attitudes of Motivated High Performers

Attitude Rules OK!

It's often been said that advisers need three components to thrive – knowledge, skills and attitude. We're all guilty of focussing far too much time and energy on their first two – knowledge and skills, neglecting the pursuit of the right attitudes. All three oil the gears of a top-performing adviser, but attitude is the highest grade oil.

Attitude is the most essential attribute of top-performing advisers, without doubt, but the wrong attitude can be heavily damaging.

Here are the attitudes that all top-performing advisers share.

Determination

Determined advisers get what they want, and they refuse to accept defeat. Determination was made famous by Thomas Edison – the inventor of the light bulb and many other creations.

Edison was celebrated for making thousands of attempts before achieving success. He was quoted, "When I have fully decided that a result is worth getting, I go ahead with it and make trial after trial until it comes."

Assertiveness

Assertiveness in an adviser means being proactive and not reacting to events. Having a plan and driving towards this. Assertive advisers make their presence felt and thrive on competition, ultimately producing results.

Responsibility

Motivated advisers take responsibility for everything – their own business, results, successes, and failures.   They accept responsibility for errors, no blame and no excuses – they see their mistakes and correct them moving forward. They also take success and know how to celebrate and bottle this.

Inner Strength

Inner Strength means recovering from setbacks, knockdowns, and other events that cause most people to stall. "What's the worse that can happen?" is a question they might ask themselves as they quickly recover, shake off the dust and pull themselves together. Inner Strength is all about handling the self-dialogue that dominates all salespeople, the nagging voice that can put you down. Motivated high performers learn to cope with these voices and channel them towards ambition, quickly putting the past behind them.

Inner Desire

Top performers have an innate Inner Desire to achieve their goals. Firstly they set goals, turning them into compelling outcomes with strategic next actions littering their direction. Moving on to their goals, they generate their own energy. They either gain motivation from external sources or, more commonly, their internal burner within themselves. Many salespeople adopt mental rehearsal techniques taken from sports psychology, which allows them to practice the future before it happens, giving them further inner desire to win.

Self Confidence

Top-performing advisers have confidence in their own abilities; they never doubt. However, they are not arrogant or obnoxious, just confident – there's a fine line, and they don't cross it. They just know they are capable of achieving their goals.

Trust

Top-performing advisers ooze trust in others – particularly their teams that support them. They communicate well with their teams, often motivational and encouraging to others. They are good delegators to their support teams and use them appropriately.

Influencers

Top performers have a range of influencing styles that they can flex to suit the occasion. Both pull and push style influencing is used. They like to influence, find it easy, and take control of situations that require management.

Coachability

advisers that reach the top and remain so enjoy and relish coaching from a sales manager. They are good at being coached are willing and receptive to the words of a quality coach. They know how to accept feedback, quickly eliminating criticism in their minds as constructive guidance. They either take or reject the feedback and then act on it quickly and decisively…and move forward. They don't dwell on it. Today is another day, and my goals drive me forward.

www.ingramcontent.com/pod-product-compliance
Lightning Source LLC
Chambersburg PA
CBHW051210200326
41519CB00025B/7066